FAMILY, FRIENDS AND FAITH

Family, Friends and Faith: *Lessons I have Learned*

Copyright © 2019 by Mark Hecht

All rights reserved.

ISBN: 9781095786864

A publication of Pulpit to Page || A division of Tall Pine Books

PULPITTOPAGE.COM || TALLPINEBOOKS.COM

Cover photography by Tawni Betts

*Printed in the United States of America

FAMILY, FRIENDS AND FAITH

LESSONS I HAVE LEARNED

MARK HECHT

To those who have walked ahead of me...
my parents John and Annie

To the one who walks with me...
the love of my life, my wife Karen

To those who follow after me...
our children John, Aaron, Annie and Joshua

ACKNOWLEDGMENTS

This book is the result of decades of blessings poured out upon my life. I am eternally grateful for the members of Hick's Memorial, the church family that raised me and nurtured my call into ministry. I remember fondly the congregations I have served over the past thirty years; Smithfield United Church, Creighton Janes UMC, Mt. Lebanon UMC, Park UMC and Warren First UMC.

After years of suggestions and nudging, I have finally responded to their prompts and have attempted to gather together a meaningful collection of messages to share. In a few cases I have changed names and combined character traits. But the spirit of each story shared is grounded in truth. I am especially thankful for the members of each of my Covenant Groups over the years who have lifted me up when I was down and have helped to remind me often why I do what I do in ministry.

Thanks also to my many colleagues who have shared their life in Christ with me. I especially thank my sister in Christ Janet Lord for her friendship and encouragement. Thank you, all!

CONTENTS

INTRODUCTION

"I was glad when they said unto me, 'Let us go to the house of the Lord!'" (Psalm 122:1)

It was the second Sunday of June 1970. Once again, like every year preceding it and many that followed, the children's Sunday School classes of my home church would lead worship for the annual Children's Day Service. The high school youth shared the liturgy, the middle school class performed several less serious skits and the grade school children sang. This particular year I was among the youngest members of the Sunday School. Our sole responsibility was to stand in front of the congregation in a single file line that stretched from the baptismal font on the left side of the sanctuary to the piano on the far right side. One by one we would each step forward to the large silver microphone in the center of the altar area. There we would recite from memory, the verse of scripture we had been assigned and had practiced for multiple weeks.

My verse was Psalm 122:1. My mother recited it to me each night before I went to bed. I said it over and over again as I ate my breakfast each morning. I needed no prompting at all from my teacher as we rehearsed our lines during the Sunday School hour prior to worship that day. I was ready!

We returned to our basement Sunday School classroom and awaited the beginning of worship. As the church organ began to play, dozens of children marched obediently up the stairs to the sanctuary and sat shoulder to shoulder crammed into the first several rows of church pews. The youngest kids were always the first to share, so after we sang the opening hymn, *Jesus Loves the Little Children,* our class made its way to the front of the sanctuary.

The church was filled. Parents and grandparents beaming with pride, pointing to their children as the kids smiled and waved back to their family members. Everyone quieted down and it was time to begin. I was fourth in line. Each of my first three classmates stumbled or paused as they spoke their line of scripture. I was not going to let that happen when it came to my turn.

I confidently walked to the microphone, cleared my throat and using my biggest *outside voice* proclaimed:

"I was glad when they said unto me, GET OFF OF THE HORSE OF THE LORD!"

The congregation burst out in laughter, I bowed and returned to my place in line, only to be told later the error I had made.

I don't know if it was the excitement of that moment, the embarrassment that followed, or simply a prompting of the Holy Spirit, but that verse has remained in my heart and has influenced my life like few others have. In fact, I might dare say that Psalm 122:1 has become a *life verse* for me. "I was glad when they said unto me, let us go to the house of the Lord!"

It was Eugene Peterson who once wrote that *"Psalm 122 is the song of a person who decides to go to church and worship God."* I was blessed to be raised in a household that valued and treasured participation in the church. Sunday morning attendance at Sunday School and worship was not suggested, it was assumed. Truly, each week the unspoken attitude of our family as we climbed into the car to drive to service was one of genuine gladness, as we went together to the house of the Lord! In many ways it was the highpoint of the week! And it was there that I was loved and nurtured into faith by parents, teachers, pastors and members of the body of Christ we call *the church*.

For as long as I can remember, the church has been my second home and the congregations I have attended and served have been my second family. As of the day I am writing this, I have preached 2513 sermons, not counting weddings, funerals and any number of impromptu talks in small groups down through the years.

I wish I could claim with absolute certainty that each of these messages "hit the mark", transformed the lives of the listener, moved individuals and congregations to places of greater love for others and commitment to their God. I wish I could write that this was the case...the reality, however, is somewhat different. As every preacher will tell you "Not every message is a *home run*."

Yet, as I reflect upon the many sermons preached and the stories I have shared over the years I have come to realize something. The messages that have most often reached the heart of the listener, made the worship attendee sit up and take notice and perhaps even nudged a few brothers and sisters in the faith to put that faith into action, all share something in common. They are the messages that include stories of my childhood and those who nurtured me in the faith, as well as the stories of my wife and our children whose faith we have attempted to nurture. Every time I come to the house of the Lord I bring with me the memories of those from my past as well as my hopes and dreams for those who follow. In a very real sense these stories serve as *songs of ascent* for my life in the church and my life in Christ.

As Christians we are on a journey and our journey is not alone. As we come together regularly as the people of God for worship, we are reminded just how much we need one another. We cannot grow in faith without others sharing their faith with us. What follows is a collection of messages that recount those touchstones from my past that have built the foundation of my life and ministry.

I pray that in reading about those who have formed my faith, you might be reminded of those who have helped to form yours. As you read of those whom God entrusted to my care you will be mindful of those who God has placed in your life to love and care for.

PART I

LESSONS THAT HAVE LASTED

In many ways our personal faith stories begin before we are even born. The lives of those who have come and gone before us touch our own as their stories are passed down through the generations. If we are fortunate enough we may have had the opportunity to hear from these persons directly. Even though they have long since passed, as we remember their stories we are blessed.

LIFE GOES ON

SUGGESTED READING: LUKE 2:29-32

C harles Dickens' *A Christmas Carol* is filled with memorable characters reciting memorable lines. From Ebenezer Scrooge's "Bah Humbug!" to Tiny Tim's "God bless us, every one!" Who isn't moved by the writing of this great author? I will admit, however, my favorite line in this Christmas classic comes from neither Scrooge or Tim or any number of other characters. Rather, my favorite line is spoken by Scrooge's faithful yet suffering employee, Bob Cratchit. The scene comes in the midst of Scrooge's midnight visits with the spirits of Christmas. In one such vision, the reader clearly is made to understand that Tiny Tim has died. Bob has returned home to his wife and remaining children after visiting Tim's grave. In an attempt to comfort his loved ones he says, "Life is a series of meetings and partings; that is the way of it!"

What a simple, yet powerful observation regarding life. I would further add that more often than not, the meetings bring us joy and happiness and the partings leave us saddened and perhaps even lost. This is particularly true when it comes to individuals with whom we have some intimate connection.

Have you ever taken the time to really remember those who have been a part of your life; your spouse, parents, children, brothers, sisters, family and friends? And in so doing, to acknowledge that in some way each of those lives, and your own, have been woven together through the meetings and partings that have occurred in this life.

I experienced my first meeting and parting on the campus of Allegheny College in Meadville, Pennsylvania in the fall of 1982. I admit that I didn't fully grasp the significance of that moment until many years later.

My parents delivered me to my dorm room in Edwards Hall and proceeded to walk the campus as I unpacked my room. Four years later, on my graduation day in June of 1986, my father pointed out to me the bench by Allegheny's "Old Main" building called Bentley Hall where he sat and cried my first day of college.

It wasn't until 25 years later, the day we dropped our oldest son off at Ravine Hall on the same campus to begin his freshman year at Allegheny, that I understood the mixture of pride and joy, anxiousness and trepidation that one feels for those who are part of their life when it is time to part. It wasn't long after my graduation from Allegheny that both my father and mother passed away. To this day, each time I go to the campus, I see that bench and I remember their love and their hopes and dreams for me.

A few years later I graduated from seminary, was ordained a United Methodist Minister, and was appointed to my first church in Western Pennsylvania. I was visiting the members of my new church and called this particular day on the most senior member of the congregation. Martha was over 100 years young at the time. I remember walking into her bedroom in the back of the house. On her wall was a very old sampler that shared a sentiment that I have never forgotten:

Our lives are albums written through
With good and ill, with false and true
And as the blessed angels turn the pages of our years,
God grant they read the good with smiles and blot the ill with
tears.

How fortunate each of us is to have had something and or someone touch our lives. To help make up the album that is our life. That is yet another reason we have to remember them.

From the time I was a very young child, I could remember going with my grandmother and mother every Memorial Day to the cemetery and helping to plant flowers on the graves of my grandfather, my great grandparents and my great-great grandparents. Every year we would make the trip to tend to those markers all found in one corner of Carson Valley Cemetery outside the small central Pennsylvania town of Duncansville, where I grew up. We would place our flowers, among the many others planted there, in that often visited section of the cemetery.

Then we would all walk to the other side of the cemetery to a much older and somewhat neglected section. The markers were obviously old. Many had in fact fallen over or been worn smooth with the passing years. We would proceed to a tiny little marker with the name Little Eva (1872-1886) and there we would plant one more flower before departing.

"Who was this young girl that died before her 14th birthday so many years ago?" I asked my grandmother. Grandma proceeded to tell me that Eva was one of thirteen brothers and sisters of her mother, and that she had died of tuberculosis at the age of thirteen. Over the years, Eva had seemingly been forgotten by everyone in the family. Only my great grandmother (out of a family of a dozen siblings) would go and tend to her grave. As the years passed, my grandmother took the responsibility for Eva's grave and after she too passed away, my mother and I did the same. A few short years later I would go alone. And years later still, I would take my own children and place flowers on the family graves including Little Eva.

Why did we do this? Why go to the trouble of placing flowers on the grave of a little girl separated from my own children by four generations and 140 years? For no reason other than the one my great grandmother gave my grandmother many years ago...when she told her that *"no one deserves to be forgotten."*

It is so important to remember those who have gone before us for what they have meant and will always mean to us. A number of years ago I was traveling through England and Scotland and as I was fumbling with a two pound coin one day, I looked closely at it and noticed that on the edges of the coin was written *"Standing on the shoulders of giants."*

Some attribute the line to Sir Isaac Newton who in 1676 wrote to a colleague, *"If I have seen further it is by standing on the shoulders of giants."*

I have come to truly love this quote because it reminds me that who I am and what I do and accomplish in this life is not simply about *me*. Rather, I am who I am because of those who have gone before me. My personal life has been impacted by my parents and grandmother, church members and friends who have all gone before me. All that I am and do is built upon the lives that have gone before me...they have *lifted me*.

Those who have gone before us should be remembered for what they have left with us to shape and lift us into our future. For people of faith there is yet one more reason to remember. Luke 2:29-32 KJV offers the following:

Lord now lettest thou thy servant depart in peace according to thy word: For mine eyes have seen thy salvation, Which thou hast prepared before the face of all people; A light to lighten the Gentiles, and the glory of thy people Israel.

These are the words spoken by Simeon, a great man of faith who spent his time in the temple of the Lord. When Mary and Joseph bring the baby Jesus in to be dedicated a few days after his birth only Simeon and Anna recognize Jesus for who He is. Simeon knows Jesus has been sent by God to save the world, including Simeon! Simeon accepts this and celebrates it, and because he knows Jesus, Simeon is now prepared to die. He does not fear death but welcomes it because he knows the Lord and he knows the Lord is in control. Did Simeon think, or believe, that he would die that very day? I don't believe so. When did he die? The scriptures don't tell us. They simply remind and assure us that this man of faith was ready because he had seen his Lord.

What an incredibly comforting reminder to each of us. To be able to live our lives with joy and peace because we know the way we are going. We know the way, in large part, because of those who have gone before us and shown us how to live, and sometimes, even how to die.

When I was a young boy, a favorite story of mine was the Velveteen Rabbit. The story of a toy stuffed rabbit that wanted very much to become a real bunny but didn't know if or how it was possible. At one point he seeks the advice of another one of the toys in the child's play-room...the Skin Horse. His answer regarding just what it means to be real in this life, is one that has stuck with me all these years:

"'Real isn't how you are made,' said the Skin Horse. 'It's a thing that happens to you. When a child loves you for a long, long time, not just to play with, but REALLY loves you, then you become Real.'

'Does it hurt?' asked the Rabbit.

'Sometimes,' said the Skin Horse, for he was always truthful. 'When you are Real you don't mind being hurt.'

'Does it happen all at once, like being wound up,' he asked, 'or bit by bit?'

'It doesn't happen all at once,' said the Skin Horse. 'You become. It takes a long time. That's why it doesn't happen often to people who break easily, or have sharp edges, or who have to be carefully kept. Generally, by the time you are Real, most of your hair has been loved off, and your eyes drop out and you get loose in the joints and very shabby. But these things don't matter at all, because once you are Real you can't be ugly, except to people who don't understand.'" *(source: **Margery Williams Bianco,** The Velveteen Rabbit)*

How important it is to remember the *real* lives of those we *love*. Friends and family who are as real to us today as they ever were.

The poet, Robert Frost once wrote, "In three words I can sum up everything I've learned about life: IT GOES ON!" We live lives filled with memories of *meetings and partings,* remembering those who are no longer with us, except in memory. Celebrating the influence they have had on us. Acknowledging we are the album upon which the lives of *giants* have been written. And yes, acknowledging also, that our loss is real but confident that those we love have gone on ahead of us and we commit to doing the same. And Life goes on. Thanks be to God. *Amen*.

2

DEAR FRIEND ANNIE

SUGGESTED READING: I THESSALONIANS CHAPTER 5

I t was the year 1899. Judy Crichton, in her book *America 1900: The Turning Point* offers the following description of the time period:

THERE WAS GREAT DEBATE AS TO WHETHER JANUARY 1, 1900 was the first day of the new century, or simply the beginning of the last year of the old. President William McKinley, Queen Victoria of England, and Pope Leo the Thirteenth, were all quite certain that the twentieth century was still one year away, but in Berlin on New Year's Eve, the German Emperor, Kaiser Wilhelm, hailed the birth of the new century with a 33 gun salute.

In the weeks leading up to January 1, 1900, newspaper articles were written and sermons were delivered summing up the wonders of the nineteenth century. The New York Times reported, "The 19th century had been marked by greater progress in all that pertains to the material well-being and enlightenment of mankind than all the previous history of the race." The Washington Post declared, "In every department of scientific and intellectual activity, we have gone beyond the wildest dreams of 1800." By the end of the 19th century discoveries in medicine, had greatly extended life. It was not uncommon for American men to expect to reach 48 years of age. Women could count on reaching 51. (Crichton pages 3-5)

In early 1898 my great grandfather, George Washington Asbury Kantner (he preferred to go by Asbury) volunteered for military service. The Spanish American War had begun and responding to cries of "Remember the Maine", Asbury, like so many others, was preparing to go to war.

One of the great treasures of my family is a series of approximately 50 letters sent from Asbury to his then girlfriend Annie, over the next three years. In these letters is the story of two persons living at the end of one century and living into the next. The correspondence begins in early 1899 from Jefferson Barracks, Missouri where Asbury's regiment received training.

It continues from New York City from where Asbury and his regiment were to ship out. In New York he is taken ill, hospitalized and must remain behind as his regiment made its way to the Philippines.

Over a period of several weeks recovery he continued to write to Annie and by September of that year he found himself in the Philippine Islands as the war ended and the Philippine occupation began. Letters home continue, until his discharge in late 1901. What follows are a few excerpts from those letters:

∾

BEDLOE'S ISLAND NEW YORK, MARCH 17TH, 1899

Dear Friend Annie,

I received your kind and ever welcome letter today. I was glad to hear that you were enjoying good health. Your letter found me the same. But I am not content here for soon I expect to join my regiment. I think we will have the privilege to leave here. In a month the next regiment leaves this country and I expect to be with them.

I am having some good times. I can go to New York every day. I was there yesterday. A day in New York is worth a year of schooling to a person, for there is a lot to be seen. I often go to the Statue of Liberty. I suppose you have heard that it is 300 feet high! I was in the top of it several times. From the top I can see all the big boats that come to New York. It is certainly a sight to be over at the immigrant buildings. The immigrants landing there are jammed up and kept until friends or family come after them. Annie you spoke of my picture. I wrote home about it and they told me they had given them all out. I was sorry to hear that for I wanted you to have a have one of them. Rob has one in Manila and I am going to write him and tell him to send it back and then you will get it. I'm going to get my picture taken in my uniform before I leave here and then I will send you one of them also.

Annie I don't know whether I will get to come home or not but we're going through Altoona and hope I may have the pleasure of seeing you before I go east. You spoke of the letter you wrote after I had left Missouri. I did not get it and suppose it's on its way to Manila. The mail that came for me was put on the boat, but that is fine, for when I arrive there I will have the pleasure of reading it. I am always anxious to read a letter from you. As news is scarce I bring this scribbling to a close.

I remain your true friend,

Asbury

BEDLOE'S ISLAND. NEW YORK APRIL 4TH 1899
Dear Friend Annie,

I received your kind and ever welcome letter today and was glad to hear from you and glad to know that you are getting better for it is a very unpleasant thing to be sick. Annie we are going to leave here on the 14th of this month for San Francisco and expect to get to Altoona the evening of the 15th and I will be very glad to have the pleasure of seeing you there.

We had a hard time here last week as a boatload of dead soldiers were brought in from Cuba. That was certainly a sight. Their mothers and sisters were here, claiming the boys as they were brought off the boat. That was a sight I do not want to witness again soon. A person could hardly walk through the streets a week after the boat landed. As news is scarce I will bring the scribbling to a close. Please excuse bad writing and mistakes.

I remain your true friend,
Asbury

DE LA PAZ, PHILIPPINE ISLANDS. DECEMBER 1899
Dear Friend Annie,

I take great pleasure in writing you from this far off country and informing you that I am enjoying good health and hope that when these few lines reach you they will find you the same. As we are going to leave this town and go to parts unknown, I don't think I will have a chance to write again for some time. As we got orders to get ready for a three-month campaign, we will be on the go all the time, but I think by the time our three-month tour is up the war will be over.

Well Annie, by the time you get my letter you will be preparing for Christmas. I only wish I could be home to spend it with you as I know I would enjoy myself. But I guess there is no use wishing as I don't think I will have a chance to spend Christmas at home for a year. I do wish you a Merry Christmas and Happy New Year, if I cannot enjoy it myself I hope you will.

There is talk that they are going to send us home in about six months to get ready to go to Paris to the World's Fair. I don't know if there is any truth to this or not. I hope there is, as that would be a fine trip, but it seems too good to be true.

I remain your ever true friend,

Asbury Kantner

Dear Friend Annie,

We had a nice time at Christmas. We had an invitation to a native dance. We certainly did enjoy ourselves but then a day like that only comes once a year. They had a big-time on that day. The people start to dance in the morning and it lasted until the next day. I do hope I will have the pleasure of being with YOU next Christmas as I know we would enjoy ourselves.

It has been nearly two years since I have been in civilization. I will be very glad when my time is up to get back to the U.S. again. I have a little over ten months to do yet, but then that will not seem long as some of us are having a pretty easy time here now. I was surprised to hear of so many getting married. If they keep on they will all be married by the time I am sent home and I will be left. But then if they all do like Lemo Martin, there will still be a chance. I don't think there are very many in town as worthless as he is, for a man that would break an oath, as he did, is not fit for a husband.

Annie you wrote of not having any snow there yet, but I suppose by this time you have seen plenty. Here we never have any snow. It's the same the whole year-round. I'm nearly crazy to get a sleigh ride, but then I will make it up to you next *winter when I get home. I suppose you enjoy sleigh rides for there are very few who don't.*

   Your True Friend,
   Asbury

   Dear Friend Annie,

   I received your kind and ever welcome letter this afternoon and was more than glad to hear from you and to learn that you are enjoying good health. Your letter has found me the same. I have never enjoyed life better than I do at present. If it only lasts, but health is very uncertain over here. You may be in fine health one day and sick the next, but a person must put up with sickness wherever they are.

   I was glad to hear that you enjoyed the Fourth. As for myself, I had a very pleasant time in Manila, but I was wishing I could spend the Fourth with you. As I know I would have a better time with you, but then as my time is getting so close it will not be long until we can have some pleasant times together.

   Annie I am very thankful to you for making calls on my grandmother as I know she gets very lonely at home and is getting too old to go visiting. I guess Charlie Garland has arrived by this time and I suppose he has some great tales to tell. When I get home I will tell you what I forgot to write as I am somewhat better at talking than I am at writing. I will say goodbye hoping to hear from you soon. From your ever true friend.

   My Love To You,
   Asbury Kantner

~

ASBURY WAS SOON DISCHARGED AND ASBURY AND ANNIE WERE *married in July of 1902.*

Did you notice what was missing from those letters from the close of the 19th century? In the entire collection of letters there was not a single reference to the fact that the century was ending. Instead, the correspondence contained stories of real people caught up in living real life, with little time to worry about or express interest in the ramifications of passing from one century to the next. Now, would you call that an optimistic or pessimistic view of life?

At first glance Paul's letter to the church in Thessalonica, seems to encourage almost a pessimistic attitude towards life in general for those who follow Christ Jesus.

For you yourselves know very well that the day of the Lord will come like a thief in the night.

According to numerous surveys, both youth and adults, when asked what their major or primary concern in life is currently, respond with answers related to crime and safety issues. We no longer feel safe in our homes, our schools, our streets or our churches. The fear of the thief, the uncertainty of *if and when he will strike* is terrifying people today.

When the thief comes it is not a time to celebrate but a time to fear and tremble. The day of the Lord, that Paul writes of, is likewise not a day of rejoicing so much as it is a day of judgment. The term *"day of the Lord"* is the same terminology used by God to Noah as judgment was about to be distributed upon the people. Likewise, the same language was used in regards to Sodom and Gomorrah before their destruction.

The *day of the Lord* will come. It will be a time of judgment and many will be fearful.

Paul goes on to write, *"When they say there is peace and security then sudden destruction will come upon them as labor pains come upon a pregnant woman and there will be no escape."*

The image of labor pains is symbolic again of the suddenness and unrelenting pain that will follow the coming of the day of the Lord. Just as it is inevitable that once labor pains begin they will continue until the baby comes...so too is it inevitable that once the pains of judgment begin they will not cease until they come to their conclusion.

To be sure, to this point Paul's cup would certainly seem to be half empty, but then the attitude of his letter seems to switch gears.

"But you beloved are not in darkness for that day to surprise you like a thief, for you are all children of light and children of the day; we are not of the night or of darkness." (1 Thess 5:4)

In the early first century there was a religious group from the east that held similar beliefs to the early Christians. They were known as Zoroastrians, and like Christians, they believed that there were powers of good and evil in the world. The *good* were referred to as powers of light and the *evil,* of course, were the powers of darkness. Like the Christians they believed the leaders behind these powers to be basically the equivalent of God and Satan.

What differentiated them from the Christians was their belief that God and Satan were absolutely equal in power and that therefore the battle between good and evil would continue forever in the world without an end. Can you imagine an existence in which good would never prevail and the best you could hope for in life was a draw?

For these people, the world was a pretty sad place,

there was literally no hope that peace and love might ever reign. The best one could hope for was a cup half-full, a world half-saved and a life half-lived.

Christians then, as we today should also realize, knew that ultimately the battle would be won. They knew that evil was not equal to goodness. They knew that the day of the Lord would come one day. Goodness would prevail and judgment would come to those in darkness.

When Paul writes that *we belong to the day*, he is reminding the people that when we accept Christ we accept the fact that His kingdom will come and that His will shall be done. Paul writes:

"So then let us not fall asleep as others do, but let us keep awake and be sober; for those who sleep at night and those who are drunk get drunk at night." (I Thess 5:6)

He is telling the Christian that along with accepting Christ into your life comes the responsibility of living a right life for Christ's sake, and that to do this properly one must be diligent and alert at all times.

In other words, to faithfully serve your Lord, you must be ready, willing and able, at any moment to respond to His call upon your life. If you have things in your life that distract you, be forewarned of the possible consequences.

How true these words are for us even today. We live in a world of addiction and addictive behaviors. Movie stars die from drug overdoses, star musicians and athletes go to rehabilitation for alcohol addiction, tobacco is a leading cause of death among women today. Teenage girls are starving themselves to death to achieve the proper look.

Children are watching over 40 hours of television a week and perhaps spending equal time on their cell phones. Children are killing children in our city streets and it will not be long until it happens in our very own neighborhoods! Then the cries "We didn't think it could happen here!" will be heard.

What all these things have in common is that they cause us to lose our focus on what is really important in this life and world. Paul, two thousand years ago, had an answer for the problem. He said:

But since we belong to the day let us be sober, and put on the breastplate of faith and love and for a helmet, the hope of salvation through our Lord Jesus Christ, Who died for us so that whether we are awake or asleep we may live with Him. (1 Thess 5:8 CSV)

Did you notice the military images? A *breastplate* of faith and love, a *helmet* of hope of salvation. Paul recognized something that we don't always recognize today which is that dealing with these issues is like going to battle...in fact, *it is war!*

If we are going to conquer these issues in our society, and we can, we must be willing to fight the battle. Spiritual armor is a necessary defense against spiritual assaults. It is time that we who claim to follow a risen Savior, take seriously the fact that along with *acceptance* comes *responsibility.* Is there any aspect or area of your life that leaves you unprepared for the day of the Lord? Do you find yourself spending more time, energy and money on things that gratify and satisfy the flesh, rather than in areas like prayer and study that fulfill us spiritually and emotionally?

Is a child that grows up in front of a TV, 10 hours a day, ready for the world when he or she gets to school? Is an adult that depends on drugs to motivate him or herself, and still more drugs to calm him or herself down, ready for the real world either? No! And what of all the other areas of our own lives that we cling to in hopes of finding satisfaction and fulfillment? In reality we all have addictions that threaten to get between us and our God.

You know, especially in these challenging times when there seems to be so much unrest, hatred, war, and distrust...it is not uncommon to hear someone raise the issue as to whether or not we are living in the *last days*.

Isn't it ironic that we spend so much time debating whether these are indeed the last days, while almost overlooking the simple question, *"Are we ready when the day of the Lord does come?"* Are we prepared for *that day*? Have we cleared away the things in our own existence that tend to get between ourselves and our God? If we would spend more time on that question, it wouldn't matter if the world ended tomorrow, next week, next month or in a thousand years, for regardless of when it happened we would be ready! We would remain children of the light.

I admire the fact that Asbury and Annie didn't seem so concerned about dates as they did about life as it was happening. Concern for friends and family, work and devotion. Lives devoted to living in the moment, enjoying it, celebrating it and, I believe, thanking God for it. For in the long run such an attitude prepared them for a long and happy life together with one another and with God.

Think of it this way...Christ is ever at the door of our hearts. He may knock today or tomorrow, but in any case, one day He will knock. Will we be ready to answer Him when He calls?

How can we prepare, how can we lift ourselves out of the addictions of this life? Here again Paul had the answer, *"Therefore encourage one another and build up each other as indeed you are doing"* (1 Thess 5:11).

We cannot do it alone. That means when the TV set is turned off and the cell phone is set aside, the parent must be there to play with and talk to their children. When the drugs are stopped, the friend must be there to hold the hand and wipe the brow.

What this means as Christians is that we must be willing to lean on others and at the same time, allow others to lean on us. We fight this war *together*!

The good news to us all is that the living God holds the keys to the gates of hell and death and because He lives we too shall live...*Amen*!

3

THE BROKEN PICTURE FRAME
SUGGESTED READING: LUKE 15:11-32

I remember just where it sat. In the far corner of her living room. Near the doorway to the downstairs apartment. On an old three foot high metal book shelf. From my earliest recollections of places and things as a child it was there. It always sat on the top shelf on the far left side of the bookcase in the comer of the room. There must have been a half dozen other photos on that shelf. Grandma rotated them frequently. Pictures of long dead family members were replaced by the pictures of grand-children in football, band, and Boy Scout uniforms. Yes, each photo would have its moment in the sun, for a desig-nated period of time, but eventually like all the others, it would be replaced with yet another on Grandma's shelf of honor.

That is, every one except this one. This one was differ-ent. This one never moved. A picture of two little girls, in ballerina outfits. One no older than eight years old, the other, no more than seven. It sat angled in the comer of that room, by the doorway of her apartment. It was the first thing anyone who entered the room for the first time would spot. Because of its location and subject matter, it was always the last object in the room to catch your eye as you left.

A photo of two sweet little girls, from a time long ago on the day of a dance recital. This photo alone was unique, for it never moved from its spot in all of our collective memories. There was, however, something else about this picture of two young girls that set it apart from the others in Grandma's apartment. It was unlike the photos of long dead relatives in dark polished wood frames and energetic grandchildren displayed in shiny new metal ones.

The picture of these two little girls, was displayed in the same old, tarnished frame for as long as anyone could remember. But more importantly, anyone who ever viewed this frame noted the large deep crack in the glass that made its way from the top of the frame to the bottom. The line created from the splitting of the glass, divided the photo almost exactly in two. One little girl on one side and one on the other. And though the girls were seated side by side, the cracked glass made it appear as though they were two separate photos. Yes, this broken picture frame and its contents held a place of honor for many years.

No one seems to remember how or when the glass was broken, some even assumed it had always been that way. Somehow I doubt that. As a young child I often wondered why we never visited my aunt and her family even though they only lived at the other end of town (a whole four blocks away.) And the fact that when they would pick grandma up at our house, no one ever entered the home or said a word. In church our family sat in the fourth pew in the center, theirs in the third pew to our left. Again such a short distance and no one ever spoke. So close and yet again, so very far. It was obvious there was a crack in the relationship that divided these two and their families. Two little girls seated side by side, and yet separated by years and circumstance.

How did it happen? How was it that two smiling young girls could grow into silent mature adults? What horrible event could have taken place to bring about such division? The reality is that there was no one single earth shattering, frame breaking event. Suffice it to say, that these two young girls, in time took different paths in life, made different decisions, found different priorities. In short, they grew apart. They separated themselves from each other until the point when the differences in who they had become were so great that neither recognized the need for the other.

They may not have, but their mother did. I am certain friends told her she should make her daughters act differently, she should point out to them that if they cared about her, they would kiss and make up. That her life could be so much happier and complete if only the children she loved would attempt to love each other.

Yes, she could have done these things but she didn't. She never complained about them and never argued with them. Neither did she ever give up, for a parent's love for their children is an amazingly resilient and incredibly patient love.

Instead she waited and waited. I suspect all the while hoping and longing for the day when they might be reconciled, when the family might be made whole again. For years and years, decade after decade it did not happen. Then in her 80th year, some 50 years after the picture was taken of two little girls on the day of their first dance recital, this patient and loving parent died.

Some might hear such a story and think it sad for a parent to watch their children for so long, recognizing their problems and unwillingness to come together. To die without ever seeing a change. But friends this is not such a story, for their mother's death accomplished something that her life could not. It brought her daughters together. In mourning together, a new relationship was formed. There was recognition by both of all their mother had done for them. Also, I believe, a recognition of all that they had done to each other. A change took place. I won't try to tell you that all was perfect, for it wasn't, but the doors had been opened and the relationship renewed.

So much so that when the older sister was diagnosed with a terminal illness only two years later, those sisters were able to spend time together and share before her passing.

Why did my grandmother keep that photo in that frame and that frame on the shelf in the corner of her apartment for all those years? Was it an expression of her pain over the division? Was it a longing for a time when things were right and all was well, even as she acknowledged the brokenness of her world? Was it a reminder to those same girls, now grown women that the time had come to resolve such differences that divide? Perhaps it was a little bit of all these things. But more so, I believe it was an acknowledgement of the way things are in life, as well as a hope for what might yet be!

There is so very much in this life that separates us from one another and from our God. One of the most common statements made at the time of a divorce is that "we just grew apart." And before you realize what has happened a relationship is over. The reality is that it doesn't just happen. We make conscious choices in this life to go down one path or the other. At work, or in relating to our neighbors, envy often makes its way into our lives, as we wish we had what they have and resent them for it. Again, separating us from one another. It happens in relationships between the sexes. I don't understand women...I don't understand men. And it's not very long until men are from Mars and women are from Venus, literally worlds apart.

Around the globe it happens as one ethnic group battles another, as one race oppresses another. Living in the same countries, the same cities and even the same neighborhoods and proclaiming *we do not know one another.*

The reality of this life is that we are far too quick to seek out, or at the very least *accept,* separation and division. We are far slower to work towards making things whole once more. Do you believe that God is pained by such division? Does God long for a time when things were right and all was well, even as the brokenness of life is acknowledged? Does God seek out the prodigals and their brothers and sisters in this life challenging them to resolve the differences that divide? I believe that God has and continues to do this very thing.

The most important fact for us to remember is that our parent, God, was willing to die in order that we might be made whole once more. His death on a cross offers each of us the opportunity for the broken relationships of this world to be healed. Is there brokenness in your life? Do you feel separated from God or from someone else? Whether it be great or small, something that has happened recently in the spur of the moment, or festered and grown over the years, consider again the amazing fact that a Heavenly Parent patiently watches and waits to help mend the breach, heal the wound and welcome you home.

In our home today sits a photo in a new frame with new glass. The picture of two smiling girls, seated side by side separated by nothing but held together by their parent's love. The love of God, our Heavenly Parent can do the same for us. *Amen.*

4

WHEN WRESTLING WAS REAL

SUGGESTED READING: GENESIS 32:22-32

Her name was Clara Williams. A woman well into her 80's, who lived on the first floor of an old two-story home in Duncansville, Pennsylvania. My grandmother lived on the second floor and had shared the home with Clara for many years. And while it has been almost fifty years since she passed away, I can still remember Clara and her apartment as if it were yesterday. Clara was a tiny woman who bore an uncanny resemblance to the actress Irene Ryan, who played Granny on the Beverly Hillbillies.

I remember as a young boy walking down the dark steep staircase from my grandmother's apartment to Clara's. The curtains were almost always pulled, a large glass jar filled with colorful hard candy sat on the coffee table and the place always smelled of butter. Each time I would descend those stairs I would find Clara seated at the far end of her living room in her large, high backed red leather chair. The television at the other end of the room would be blaring loudly and if it were Saturday, Clara would be watching her favorite show, professional wrestling. I can still remember the likes of Bruno Sammartino, Dominic DeNucci, Stan "The Man" Stasiak, and Killer Kowalski, tumbling across her television screen as Clara cheered and booed their every move.

"Come over here and sit down and watch *my wrestlers* with me." As she would refer to them.

"Get him! Be careful watch behind you, look out for the folding chair!" she would yell at the screen on a weekly basis. This of course was in the days before promoters and wrestlers themselves would openly admit that the winners and losers of such matches were predetermined and the matches themselves highly choreographed.

Even though it was seemingly obvious to many that professional wrestling was something less than it claimed to be, Clara could never be convinced. Of course as a little boy I had no reason to believe any differently.

Of all the matches we watched and all the comments Clara ever made about *her wrestlers*, the statement I can still remember to this day was her complaint that even though she liked *them,* they were never as good as those she watched back in the fifties, like Gorgeous George and others. *"That's when wrestling was real!"* she would tell me *"Those guys weren't afraid of anything!"*

It is fifty years later, Clara long ago passed away, and the entire world knows that professional wrestling is fixed. But as I consider the story of the life of Jacob and in particular his wrestling with God, I can't help but remember the comment of Clara's that has remained with me for all this time. *"That's when wrestling was real...those guys weren't afraid of anything."*

Fear is an interesting emotion and response, don't you agree? Fear sometimes makes a person act, by running away or intentionally avoiding someone or something. When I was a little boy, I was afraid of cemeteries. Every time we would drive past one, I would hide my head in the back of the car, thinking that if I didn't see it, it didn't actually exist. However, I can assure you that not once was I actually able to make a cemetery disappear by my actions. Similarly, in July of 2000 as we were preparing to leave the congregation we had been serving in Pittsburgh, the young daughter of a dear friend told her mother that she didn't want to go to church, because if she didn't go that day, we wouldn't leave. Fortunately her mother was able to convince her otherwise, I was glad she was there. Yes, avoidance is certainly a typical response to fear.

On other occasions, fear *paralyzes us*. Freezes us in our tracks. We've all heard the expression, *frozen like a deer caught in the headlights*, a phrase that reflects what I am saying. We are afraid to move right or left, we simply stand frozen where we are.

When it comes right down to it, I believe most people are afraid of three things in this life; *moving ahead, falling behind, and standing still.* Think about it, there is uneasiness associated with being out in the lead, always worried who is gaining on you. Someone once joked that you should be kind to the people you meet on your way up the ladder because you will see them again on your way down. We are reminded time and again that success and fame can be fleeting and we should be prepared for the inevitable.

So too there is fear in falling behind. The feeling that you will never be able to catch up. Then there is always the fear of standing still, being in the middle, where complacency sets in. I'm reminded of the story of the stranger who encountered a farmer sitting on his porch overlooking his farm one early July day:

"'How's your cotton coming?'

'Ain't got none,' came the answer. 'Didn't plant none. Was afraid of the boll weevil.'

'How's your corn?'

'Didn't plant none, afraid of the drought.'

'How about your potatoes?'

'Ain't got none. Scared of the tater bugs.'

Finally the stranger asked, 'Well what did you plant?'

'Nothin', answered the farmer, 'I just played it safe this year.'"

Fear that causes us to do nothing at all is perhaps the worst possible fear of all.

Some of us also fear that what we have done in the past will catch up with us. The author of Sherlock Holmes, Sir Arthur Conan Doyle, once played a practical joke on twelve men regarded as pillars of the establishment in England. He sent each of them a telegram, with the same message in each: "Flee at once. All is discovered." Within twenty-four hours, they had all fled the country! Virtually all of us have something in our lives of which we are ashamed; something we would not want everyone to know about. We often put up barriers around us to avoid the possibility of being found out.

When it comes to dealing with the subject of fear, Jacob is a very helpful example to consider. Jacob had been a man whose life was consistently impacted by how he chose to deal with critical events.

Let's briefly review the life of Jacob to this point. Remember that Jacob was the second born son of Isaac and because of that his brother Esau was to inherit the greater share of the property and possessions of their father. History tells us that as these twins were born, Jacob was the second, holding on to the heel of his brother. The name Jacob in fact means, *to seize by the heel,* but it also has a very interesting connotation that goes along with that, which is, *to overreach* or to *take over.*

Scripture tells us that in the years to follow, Jacob would use many different means to trick his father, his brother and others to get what he wanted. Each time Jacob is either caught or nearly caught, he does not face the consequences but instead fears and runs. He tricks his brother and father for the birthright and then flees in fear that Esau will kill him.

Later he finds himself with the household of Laban, and he makes a deal to work for Laban for seven years in order to marry Rachel. After fulfilling his end of this deal, he is tricked by Laban into marrying *Leah* instead. Then, rather than standing up to Laban for what is right, he gives in to Laban and agrees to work seven more years in order to marry Rachel.

Later on in the story of Jacob, he gets the better of Laban in a deal for sheep and goats. Laban's sons want to kill Jacob so he runs away again, is overtaken by them, and makes a deal to save himself.

It would seem that time and time again Jacob has been ruled by *fear,* especially at critical points in his life.

We are told that Jacob is afraid because he receives word that Esau is coming after him with four hundred men and Jacob naturally assumes Esau is coming to destroy him. So Jacob prays to God to help him and then attempts to send a bribe to Esau to appease him.

Then for the first time, perhaps in his life, Jacob acts differently. He takes his wives and children and sends them across the river with everything that he owns. He remains on the other side of the Jabbok river alone.

The very next verse tells us, Jacob was left alone and a man wrestled with him until daybreak. After this his name is changed from Jacob to *Israel*, which means *one who strives with God.*

From that moment on, Jacob...Israel, is *changed*. He is a different man. Witness the very next story in Genesis, which tells us the next day Israel goes out ahead of his family to meet Esau face to face. He does not know what Esau will do to him, but he confidently approaches him nonetheless. As the story unfolds we find that in fact Esau does not seek to destroy his brother and the relationship is mended.

The more I have thought about it, the more I think Clara was on to something. In order to wrestle with someone or something in this life, it is essential that one is not afraid. Wrestling is real when the one who wrestles faces his or her fears.

Jacob's wrestling was oh so real, because he was not only wrestling with God but with himself. In the presence of God, Jacob recognizes just how unworthy he is. Someone once wrote "It's the consequence that comes to every soul that has tried too long to evade the truth about itself... *this* struggle in the dark."

I think everyone of us, at one time or another, has sat and thought how unworthy we are to have what we have, or to be what we are. Oftentimes these thoughts are brought on when we compare ourselves to others who have given so much to the world. Perhaps we watch a TV special or read a news article about people who have given all they have to help feed and house the poor, or who feel so committed to some cause that they are willing to sacrifice their very lives. We then look at our own lives and feel humbled, embarrassed, ashamed and afraid. Yet instead of facing those feelings and doing something about them, we run the other way.

Think of what Jacob must have felt like that night! He is not comparing himself to a mere human, but to God Himself! They struggle the whole night through and at the hour when he might have been most discouraged about himself, *a new day dawned*. Now able to recognize his shortcomings, he could begin to pass beyond them.

What is it that you fear? Getting ahead, falling behind, succeeding or failing, being remembered or being forgotten? What have you done in your life that you wish you hadn't, what have you left undone to this point that you wish you could do something about? What decisions have you made or left undecided? What do you fear? And more importantly, *what will you do about it?*

Jacob realized something at the Jabbok River thousands of years ago that is essential for Christians today to realize and understand as well. That there is nothing we can do to make ourselves worthy of the love of God. That love comes unconditionally and fully. We do not deserve it and yet it is there. No one set of actions will make that love last any longer or be any better. Certainly no amount of excuse making or stalling for time, or regret over past mistakes, is going to help either.

Charles Wesley, the brother of John Wesley who was the founder of Methodism, was known for his prolific hymn writing. He wrote over 7000 hymns during the course of his lifetime. Perhaps his greatest and also least sung hymn was entitled *Come O Thou Traveler Unknown*. Most meaningful because he uses the story of Jacob at the Jabbok river to help explain his own conversion experience. Least sung, quite frankly, because it has fourteen stanzas and does not easily lend itself to the modern day worship experience. The great hymn begins with the expression of a broken spirit wrestling with himself as well as with God.

Come, O thou Traveler unknown,
whom still I hold, but cannot see!
My company before is gone,
and I am left alone with thee;
with thee all night I mean to stay
and wrestle till the break of day.

How many others have lived through such moments of fear and uncertainty?

When Jacob wrestled with God on the bank of the Jabbok River so many years ago, that truly could have been the first professional wrestling match. Because there was never a doubt what the outcome would be. When one encounters God, one is changed. *For God is a mighty fortress, a bulwark never failing, our helper mid the flood of mortal ills prevailing.*

As God encountered Jacob, so too does God's love come freely to each of us in the person of Jesus Christ. Let's return once more to Wesley's beautiful hymn. By the time we reach the ninth stanza, after describing the depths to which one descends apart from God and the lengths to which God is willing to go to seek us out when we go astray, we come to this glorious realization

'Tis Love! 'tis Love! thou diedst for me,
I hear thy whisper in my heart.
The morning breaks, the shadows flee,
pure, Universal Love thou art;
to me, to all, thy mercies move --
thy nature, and thy name is Love.

And as we stand before the cross on which He died so that we might live, we too still wrestle. And in wrestling we too are allowing for the all excelling love of God to come down and enter every trembling heart. And in so doing we are changed.

Ask yourself this question. Have I really ever allowed myself to come face to face with my Lord and Savior! And if not, is it because I am afraid or embarrassed at how I might appear because of the things I have done or left undone? Guess what? God already knows everything that each and every one of us has done or left undone, *and still God loves us.*

All God asks is that we come to Him. And yes it may be a struggle, and yes it may take many years, as it did for Jacob. But we must do it. Like Jacob, we too can step from the despair of darkness and fear that causes us to run away and close our eyes and enter into the joy of a new day. Let us, as the hymn says, ask the loving Spirit to enter every troubled breast and take away our bent to sinning. Wrestling no longer and fearing no more, let us find our new life in Christ.

PART I DISCUSSION QUESTIONS

1. Do you have a personal *life verse*? When did it become a life verse for you and how has it influenced/shaped your life?
2. Does your family pass along the *stories* of your ancestors? Why or why not?
3. Which of your family members' lives has had the greatest influence in your faith development?
4. If you could ask one question of a deceased family member what would it be?
5. How are *faith* and *fear* opposites?

PART II

LESSONS FROM HOME

Clearly our childhood years influence us in profound ways. Much of who we become in our adult life is formed during those early years. Recounting stories of life at home and at church helps us to understand where our priorities in life come from. It is here that we first learn how to step out in faith.

HOME FOR THE HOLIDAYS
SUGGESTED READING: ISAIAH 35:1-10 AND LUKE 2:15-20

The year was 1969 and two young boys knelt and looked through the basement windows of the old church. It was cold outside that early winter evening. Although it was only 5 o'clock, the wintertime sun had already set. The light of the sanctuary, shining out through the large stained glass windows, was all that illuminated the night. The two little boys crouched down, silhouetted against the old brick building. A new layer of December snow had fallen and covered the ground with a blanket of white. It was still snowing as the two young boys peered inside that early winter's night.

From where they knelt they could spy a flurry of activity taking place in the basement of that old church building. Dozens of women were moving quickly back and forth through the church kitchen. The boys were used to seeing a lot of activity in that room but this was different. There was no meal being served this evening. And yet there was food everywhere. Bags and bags of canned goods were carried into the room and unpacked on the far counter of the old church kitchen.

Along another wall were boxes and boxes filled with oranges and apples. One by one each piece of fruit was inspected and placed back in the box until one of the women would come and collect a dozen or so of each fruit, bag and carry them to the center of the room to yet another box. Next to the boxes of fruit sat tray after tray of Christmas cookies. Sugar cookies cut into shapes of wreaths and snowmen, bells and Christmas trees. The boys watched in amazement as several more women carefully packed those cookies into small white boxes, tied them with ribbon and carried them to the center of the large busy room. Every so often one of the men of the church would enter the kitchen carrying a turkey. He would make his way to the center of the room, hand off the turkey and leave. The activity in the kitchen was energized. Everyone was quickly going about his or her job. They were laughing. You could hear some of them singing Christmas carols. The boys' mother and father were among the busy workers, scurrying about the old church basement.

At the center of that large room, stood several women who were acting differently from the rest. While everyone else was quickly darting back and forth and side to side, hand delivering canned goods, turkeys, fresh fruit and cookies, these three ladies at the center of that room, stood calmly behind large empty boxes and gently placed all the other items, one at a time, into their boxes. Canned goods went in first, a turkey next, fruit on either side, a white box filled with Christmas cookies and tied with a bow carefully positioned on top of the box and then hard Christmas candies and candy canes were sprinkled over the entire contents of the package. Very carefully large sheets of red or gold cellophane were pulled over the sides of the boxes and tied together at the top with long flowing ribbon.

The two boys were awestruck by the entire spectacle. Never had they seen so much food. And never had they witnessed such care being placed into wrapping and preparing such beautiful packages. When each box was finished it looked like a treasure chest to the young boys. As they watched the adults go about their work that night, they talked with each other about where these wonderful packages must be going. It was obvious that they were very special, so the boys reasoned that they must be presents for very important people. After all, it wasn't just *anyone* who deserved to receive such a beautiful present. Whoever it was that was going to receive those boxes, the one thing the boys did agree upon was that they must be very lucky!

It was not long until the boy's father and mother finished their work and came outside to find the brothers and make their way home; some six blocks away. The boys quickly told their parents what they had witnessed and how they wished that one day they too might receive a beautiful gift like the ones their parents were helping to prepare.

It was at that moment that their father explained to them that the people who were going to receive those large boxes of food were not the wealthy and powerful, but rather families in need in their church and small town. It was then that the boys' father...*my father,* said to his sons, *"The real joy of Christmas comes in sharing one's best with those who need it most!"* We all went home that night thankful for the experience.

Memories of Christmas. Aren't they wonderful? Thinking about years past, the way things were. What was, as well as what is today, and even what might have been. Christmas is very much about memories and about being home for the holiday.

We know that more people call home on Mother's Day than any other day of the year. Likewise it is a fact that more people travel home for Thanksgiving than any other holiday of the year. However, I would contend that it is *Christmas,* that in fact brings us home like no other holiday ever can. It is at Christmas that we remember who we are and where we came from. We remember the gifts our grandparents made for us when we were little. We remember the trips we took to see Santa Claus at the local department store with mom and dad. We remember friends from our childhood and how we once played together building snowmen and snow forts in our yards until it was so cold that we couldn't stand it any longer. We remember sledding, caroling, letters to Santa and visits to elderly relatives. Many of us spend time during this holiday remembering friends and loved ones who are no longer with us, except in our hearts.

Yes it is true that more calls are made and more travel done at other times of the year, but it is Christmas that really brings us home again. Not in a physical sense but a spiritual one. It is Christmas that helps us to remember who we are and *Whose* we are!

I don't know about you, but I believe I am more in touch with my roots at Christmas time than any other. There are more family memories associated with this season, than any other time of year. We use the decorations our parents used when we were younger and remember how they looked in our homes growing up. We spend time using the same recipes our mothers did to make the holiday cookies, so we can even *taste* our past.

And though we may not have realized it at the time, those who went before us shared what they had and who they were with us because they loved us. If we were to be honest, we do not always remember things exactly the way they really happened. Time has a way of smoothing over the difficulties and disagreements, allowing us to remember only the joy and love that was there.

The real joy of Christmas comes in sharing one's best with those who need it most! Our God knew that. For this is in fact what God did that first Christmas when He sent the baby Jesus into the world. The world did not even recognize it at the time and yet our collective memories of the story that has been passed down for two thousand years of a Baby in a manger come to save us from our sins, help us to be brought home again as well.

Only the home that I speak of now is not the home of our youth or the homes we live in today. Rather the home we are called to is a home with our Lord.

The Scripture verses from Isaiah, are words that paint a beautiful picture of the final kingdom in which God will establish justice and destroy all evil. These words speak of a time when the glory of the Lord will be seen by all. When the weak will be made strong, the blind will see, the deaf will hear, water will spring forth in the desert. No longer will the ferocious beasts be found, but the redeemed will return to the Lord. They will enter Zion with singing. Gladness and joy will overtake them and sorrow and sighing will flee away.

Now when Isaiah speaks these words he is speaking to a people who have endured hardship at the hands of their enemies and who will continue to do so. He is speaking to a people who have never known the complete peace and joy to which he refers. His is not so much a memory as it is a wish, or goal, for people of faith. A wish for what might be for the people of faith, to come home to Zion and worship the Lord.

The person of Jesus Christ makes such peace possible. *The real joy of Christmas comes in sharing one's best with those who need it most!* When we remember the Christ Child, we remember a God of love, who is willing to give us far more than we deserve. For we are still a people who need the forgiveness and salvation that Jesus Christ alone offers.

We are truly blessed, and Christmas helps us to recognize that fact like no other time. I came to this realization very early in my own life, in fact it was the Christmas of 1970. A year when my father was laid off from work for several months before the holiday and still had no full time job prospects for the future. It was that Christmas that I remember going to the front door of our house and seeing a large cellophane wrapped box of food from a church family that was *sharing it's best with those who needed it most!*

And when I remember that Christmas I am brought home for the holidays. For when I remember that gift, I remember too, the reason it was given was because a far greater gift was shared with us all in Jesus Christ.

What are your memories? What have you received that brings you home? And more importantly, what might you share with another, to help them know that their God remembers them and desires for them to come home to Him?

The real joy of Christmas comes in sharing one's best with those who need it most! Share your joy. Share your Savior. And welcome home. *Amen.*

6

TEN FOOT JESUS

SUGGESTED READING: JOHN 10:11-18 AND PSALM 23

You walked down the steps into the dark, oldest, section of the church where the youngest classes of the primary Sunday School department met each Sunday morning. The kindergarten class, first and second, and third and fourth grade classes all met there. Pressed wood dividers separated the circles of little wooden chairs where each class gathered. The classroom space looked pretty much like every other church basement in the late 1960's I suppose. But with one distinction.

When you first came down the steps and entered the primary department, hanging on the wall in the middle of the room, was the biggest picture of Jesus I had ever seen. When I was very little I could have sworn it was at least 4 feet wide and 10 feet tall! It was Jesus the Good Shepherd tending His sheep. He was standing there, holding a lamb in one arm with the other sheep in the background. As a little boy, the picture scared the living daylights out of me! It was like that picture of George Washington in our classrooms in elementary school. Remember those pictures? Wherever you stood or sat in class, it looked like President

Washington was looking at you! But this was *much worse.* Not only did it appear as though Jesus was always watching you, wherever you stood, but this Jesus had feet and arms *and He was carrying a big stick*!

To this day, I am uncertain as to what type of guilty conscience I had as a young boy that made me so uncomfortable with that picture. But I do remember that as I grew older, the picture no longer frightened me. Instead I began to find great comfort in the fact that this larger than life Jesus was watching over us. Every week when I returned to church I was reminded again and again that the Good Shepherd was there.

How was it that even as a young child, I began to see Jesus in a new light? Not as someone to fear but someone Who loved me and cared for me?

I believe I can explain it using the often spoken *call and response* in the church...

God is Good! All the time!

All the time! God is Good!

I know that God is good all the time, because that is His very nature. Jesus assures us, "I am the Good Shepherd, the Good Shepherd lays down His life for the sheep."

King David repeatedly states in various Psalms, as he does with such confidence and assurance in Psalm 106:1

"Praise the Lord! O give thanks to the Lord, for He is good; for His steadfast love endures forever."

God is good, all the time, because *His steadfast love endures forever*—even through hurricanes; even despite all terrorist attacks, wars, floods, car crashes, cancers, sicknesses and separations. Whatever hard time or tragedy may come my way—God's steadfast love endures and abides with me forever; He is good to me all the time. God is good, regardless of whether times are good or bad for us as His disciples, and the scriptures affirm that beyond any doubt. Many times we American Christians are tempted to praise God when things go our way, but refrain from praise when the going gets tough.

If you like musicals, I am sure you are familiar with the famous words that open the Rodgers and Hammerstein musical Oklahoma:

Oh, what a beautiful morning,
O what a beautiful day;
I've got a beautiful feeling
Everything's going my way.

The thing is, in our heart of hearts, *we know that everything doesn't always go our way.* So how can God be good all the time? That is the wrong question to ask. I am reminded of a country and western song first recorded by Lynn Anderson in 1970. The refrain continually reminds us:

I beg your pardon,
I never promised you a rose garden.
Along with the sunshine,
There's gotta be a little rain sometimes.

Things do not always go our way, *but God is good, all the time.* Our Good Shepherd stands on His never-ending promise to us in His closing words in Matthew 28:20, "And remember, I am with you always, to the end of the age."

As a disciple of Jesus Christ, however, I have no doubt that even when things *are not* going my way, *God is good, all the time.* You may be tempted to ask, "Mark, just how can that be so?" Do you remember those powerful words from the 23rd Psalm?

Though I walk through the valley of the shadow of death, I will fear no evil, For You are with me.

Several years ago I was attending the Kingdom Bound Christian music festival, near Buffalo, New York, with youth from our church. In addition to the great Christian musicians who shared their talents and witness, attendees had the opportunity to hear from many well-known Christian speakers during the week as well. One day, I was seated in the worship tent with a few hundred other people listening to counselor and author Kevin Leman, when something amazing happened.

Into the worship tent they came and sat right in front of me! Yes, what appeared to be a pair of conjoined, Siamese twins, connected at the head sat directly in front of me. The even more curious thing was that they were male and female. I remembered enough from my biology class in school to know that this was impossible, but there they were, sitting together for the whole time, head to head.

No matter what else was happening around them, they did not move. Others were clapping and laughing, ... there they sat. Finally, at the close of the lecture, the young man stood up and turned to his girlfriend and gave her a kiss as they went on their way. They were not joined at the head...they were in love!

But the more I think of that image, the more appropriate it is to illustrate the love of God for each of us. No matter how difficult the situations may be, whether we face trouble, hardship, persecution, famine, nakedness, danger, terrorism, war, death, demons, sickness, sorrow or pain; our Good Shepherd is *always with us. Connected!* For He affirms, again and again, throughout the Old and New Testaments, *"Never will I leave you, never will I forsake you."*

Our Good Shepherd is the One who promised Israel in Isaiah 41:10:

So do not fear, for I am with you; Be not dismayed, for I am your God. I will strengthen you and help you; I will uphold you with My righteous right hand.

That promise has not changed in more than 2700 years; and it is still true for you and me today.

It says in Romans 8:28, "And we know that all things work together for the good of those who love God, who are called according to His purpose."

My experience has been that no one goes through this life with *no* problems. Each and every one of us, at one time or another...and in some cases...one time AND another AND another AND another, face challenges and hardships.

Not all of the things that happen to us are good. Much of this is the result of human circumstances but because *"God is good, all the time,"* He uses bad circumstances *"to work for the good of those who love Him, who are called according to His purpose."*

I can certainly attest that when difficulties have arisen in my life, God has been able to take those hardships and bring about good. We all face times of trial and hardship. But let us understand that trials can indeed build character. And perhaps more importantly, by going through hard times, you and I are then prepared and strengthened to empathize with and reach out to others when they are going through difficulties. Because we have already *walked in their shoes,* we know how they feel.

It is equally important to remember that we haven't walked alone! Our Loving Good Shepherd has gone with us and because of that we can be Jesus to others, for we know that Jesus our Good Shepherd has seen us through the times we have walked through those valleys, yes, even *the valley of the shadow of death.*

Jesus is always with us and He is good, all the time! One of my favorite poets is the American Quaker, John Greenleaf Whittier. I frequently share his words at funeral services, because he so beautifully and eloquently expresses the joy that comes from knowing the Lord.

Hear what he wrote in his poem *The Eternal Goodness*:

"I see the wrong that round me lies,
I feel the guilt within;
I hear, with groan and travail—cries,
The world confess its sin.
Yet, in the maddening maze of things,
And tossed by storm and flood,
To one fixed trust my spirit clings;
I know that God is good!"

Cling to that *one fixed trust* through all the wrong you see, through all the groans and sadness. Cling to that *one fixed trust* through all the maddening mazes of life, throughout all the storms, floods, hurricanes, wars, rumors of wars, sorrow, sickness, pain, and death. Your *Good Shepherd* is with you; He will never leave you nor forsake you, for *God Is good*, all the time!

7

JOSE PAGAN #701

SUGGESTED READING: LUKE 15:1-7

Baseball cards! When I was a kid one of my favorite pastimes was to collect baseball cards. I loved going to Isenberg's Confectionary store on 3rd Avenue in Duncansville, Pennsylvania, and putting my ten cents on the counter and getting, in return, that wax paper covered stack of cards and rock hard piece of pink bubble gum that I can still smell some forty five plus years later.

I started collecting when I was only a few years old and continued until I was about 12. We didn't use protective plastic sheets and hard plastic cases to hold our cards back then. All we needed was a shoe box and a hand full of rubber bands so that we could sort our cards by teams and we would be set. Now when I think of all the different cards I had as a kid and the many years I collected, there was one year in particular that stands out far above the others as being special for a variety of reasons. The year was 1972. My team, the Pittsburgh Pirates had won the world series the year before so the Pirates team photo was the very first card in the set. I started early that spring buying, trading, flipping cards with friends to get as many of the cards as I possibly could because I wanted to make sure that I collected all the Pirates before the summer was over. Sure, I made some unwise trades. Tom Seaver for Vic Davillio, Johnny Bench for Bob Moose. But it didn't matter. The 1972 cards were also special because they were so colorful. They were great to look at and to read the back of the cards to learn about my favorite ball players.

The entire set that year included a total of 787 cards. *I was determined to get them all!* Now for many years the Topps company who produced baseball cards, released them in series of approximately 130 or so cards. This was still being done in 1972, which meant that by the time the sixth series of the season was finding its way to local stores, it was near the end of summer. By this time, thoughts had often turned away from baseball to school and other activities and this part of the set was often left incomplete in many children's shoeboxes.

By fall of 1972 I had collected almost 500 of the 787 cards. So much for a complete set. They went in the box and into the back of the closet. I didn't think much of those cards again for another 15 years. It was now 1987 and I was at seminary and one of the students there was selling a variety of items at a yard sale; lo and behold, among the many odds and ends was a box of 1972 Topps Baseball cards! Why not help him out and buy the box and see what was there? Well I did, and was able to go and find my old collection and I realized I now had close to 650 of the cards in that set. It was nice to flip through the cards and remember some of the great players of the early 70's that I liked to watch. Hank Aaron and Thurman Munson, Roberto Clemente and Willie Stargell, Willie Mays and Johnny Bench, the list went on and on, but again it wasn't all that long until the cards went back in the box and up on a shelf for several more years.

By the late 1980's old baseball cards were starting to be viewed more seriously as a collectable item and shops were popping up all over the place selling them. Periodically I would stop in and find a few more of the cards that I needed. A few minutes here and there, that seemed to bring back many fond memories, was time well spent. After all, I had collected most of the cards of star players many years before so at most, each of the additional cards I was buying were only a few cents a piece. By the mid 1990's I had found almost 730 of the 787 cards, so I went through all the cards and made a list of exactly who I still needed, and then *something very significant happened. Ebay!* Now it was no longer necessary to go door to door at card and antique shops or wait for the weekends to hit the occasional flea market or yard sale.

Ebay made it possible to find all types of items at any time of day or night, place a bid and hope for the best. So once every couple of weeks I would go online, type in *1972 baseball cards* and scan the list of those available. It didn't take long until the 57 cards I needed was down to 20 then 15 then 10. Anyone who has ever collected anything knows that as you come closer to completing a collection or set, it is natural to devote more time, energy, maybe even money to its pursuit. Again, the majority of these cards were only a few cents each so it became a relatively inexpensive hobby once again. Then on January 24th 1998 it happened. I placed a bid of 60 cents and won the last two cards #527 Dave Leonhard of the Orioles and #545 Wayne Granger of the Minnesota Twins.

After a few days the cards came in the mail and I put them in the last two slots in the album. Finally, after only

26 years of occasional interest and minimal time and monetary investment I had completed the set. And now that all the cards were in place I began to go through them and look at and read each one again. Page after page of baseball cards I turned, until *it happened*. I came to one of the last pages in the book, there was Rod Carew, Jerry Koosman, Bobby Mercer #700...but #701 JOSE PAGAN was missing! Jose Pagan, of course everyone remembers the great Jose Pagan, I am sure! A third string backup utility infielder who played 57 games and batted .241 for the 1971 Pittsburgh Pirates was *missing*! After 26 years of buying, trading, looking, waiting, and now one of my Pirates was *missing*!

787 cards in the set and *one* was missing. The set was *incomplete!* It had never bothered me before, because I had never had the complete set. Once I did, and one was missing, however, I was actually panicked. I knew exactly what I had to do. I got online again and searched the internet. Apparently the last chapter of the Jose Pagan fan club must have folded many years before. While Tom Seaver and Nolan Ryan cards were selling for large sums of money and were also readily available, Jose Pagan could not be found. Where once I would check eBay auctions every couple of days or weeks, now I would get online every night before bed and see if anybody was selling a 1972 Jose Pagan baseball card.

The search went on for weeks, and with each passing day, I was more committed than the day before to finding that card. Then it happened. Spring of 1998, a number 701 Jose Pagan card in near mint condition was up for auction on eBay. I saw it and bid - $5.00. I know that sounds like a lot for a card like that but it was the last one of 787 cards and I wanted to be sure no one else would get it. I came back later to find that bidding had taken the card to $7.00 and, not only that, ...several other people were bidding as well! Was it possible that this was the *last card* needed by a number of collectors and that *perhaps this was the last Jose Pagan card in existence*? I bid again and again. I was not going to be deterred. No way was I going to allow that card to fall into the hands of some other collector! Finally, at 27 dollars and 15 cents, it was mine.

I still remember my wife Karen's reaction the day the card came in the mail. *Look Karen the last card of the 1972 Topps Baseball set!* Her look said, *so what?*

It wasn't long after all this took place that I was reading once more the parable Jesus told about a shepherd who had lost one of his hundred sheep. For the first time I saw the story in a slightly different light.

The shepherd is not simply seeking to add one more sheep to his collection, so to speak. He has a complete set already, and one is missing. The one has even greater value, not because of the type of sheep it is, but simply because without it the set is *incomplete*. It therefore makes perfect sense that he would do whatever is necessary to find it. And not having eBay available at the time, means that he is going to have to go out on foot to make this happen.

Have you ever noticed the terminology that Jesus chooses when He expresses the fact that one of the sheep has strayed? He says, "If he has lost one of them." In the Middle East a man never blames himself for anything. (Karen says the same is true in our house!) He does not say *I missed the train,* but rather, *the train left me.* Or *I dropped the dish*, rather, *the dish broke.* Instead of *I lost the pen...the pen went from me.* Jesus does not say if one of them was lost, He clearly places the responsibility with the shepherd with that statement *if he has lost one of them*. The shepherd takes responsibility for the sheep being lost.

The shepherd is willing to pay whatever price is necessary to bring back that one sheep to the fold. A price that might seem ridiculous to others who do not have sheep, or like sheep, or ever want sheep. They look at him and his concern over the lost one that completes the set and say, *so what, you still have 99*. But not this shepherd.

It might very well take days of climbing over the rugged wilderness to find the lost sheep. But it is only when the sheep is found that the hard part would begin. The shepherd then has the task of carrying the one, back to the group. And yet the shepherd accepts this back-breaking task with joy. Whatever the cost, he is willing to pay it.

Clearly, in the eyes of the shepherd each individual sheep was precious and of worth and importance. In the sight of God everyone is precious and of worth!

A few years ago, my family had the opportunity to hear a wonderful singer-songwriter by the name of Chip Richter. Chip wrote a song entitled *He Made Me,* based upon a verse in Matthew Chapter 10.

One of the lines in that song is, *He knows the number of hairs on my head. The color of my eyes, He knows what time I go to bed and He greets me when I rise, That's because He made me, that's why I'm alive.*

We all belong to the God who created us, we are His, and together we make up an incredible collection and set. When one is missing, when one is outside of a relationship with God, when one has strayed, rebelled, been lost, confused, hurt or rejected, the God who made us is saddened. He will do whatever is necessary to find and save the lost.

Is it any wonder that Christ, the Good Shepherd was willing to come into the world and travel a very costly path to His death on a cross in order to bring us back to God? He didn't count the cost; He would give up whatever He needed to bring us back.

There is something that often is overlooked in this scripture, and that is the subtle humor that Jesus is injecting into the story. He states that there is more joy in heaven over one sinner who repents than over 99 righteous who need no repentance, when in fact there is no such group...they simply do not exist. Naturally, heaven's joy over them will be minimal. Remember Isaiah's words, *All we like sheep have gone astray.*

Just as there were other collectors bidding on the card that was so important to me, there are other collectors in this world bidding on our lives. There is evil in this world that seeks to destroy us and separate us from the One who created and loves us. Call it evil, call it sin, call it Satan himself, call it whatever you like...it is out there...and it bids for our souls again and again.

You know the times that I mean, when we become caught up in, and engrossed in our own existence at the expense of what is going on around us. We live in a world that encourages us to place priorities on things, and choose one over another. We live our lives and allow our time to be taken up with the many activities we choose for ourselves, where we become so absorbed in our job that we forget our family, and so obsessed with projects at work we forget close friends. We devote time and energy to secular concerns and allow our relationship with God to take a back seat to the concerns of this world.

This isn't just a coincidence. For there is a collector, whose intentions are not admirable, who seeks to purchase our souls. Thank God we have a Shepherd who is willing to pay the price to bring us back. And when we in fact are found, and are returned to the flock, our Shepherd is indeed in control.

There is one last characteristic of sheep that Jesus does not make reference to here but nonetheless must have been aware of. Sheep know the voice of their shepherd when he calls. Several herds can come together to graze and drink, but when their shepherd's call them, each sheep knows exactly where to go.

Sheep, and every one of us, sometimes lose our way and are in danger of being lost. Many times we don't even realize it. But if we listen for the call of the shepherd, listen for the call of the Lord, let the Shepherd take control, remembering that He has already accepted the responsibility, we, like sheep, can be returned to the fold. And *the set will be complete. Amen.*

8

"JUST SWING"

SUGGESTED READING: ACTS 3:1-20

Have you ever attempted to explain something to someone who simply had no understanding at all what you were talking about? Someone that, no matter what you said or did, agreed with you or at least pretended to agree with you, but you later realized they didn't have a clue what you were talking about.

When I was a young boy I liked to watch the old Our Gang movies on TV. A few of you reading this are old enough to remember them aren't you? A favorite episode of mine involves Spanky and Alfalfa and the rest of the boys forming the *he-man woman haters club*, because they didn't want girls around. And yet one little girl kept following Alfalfa. No matter what he said or did to discourage her, she continued to pursue him.

"Don't you know we don't want you here?" Alfalfa would say. (She would nod affirmatively.)

"Good!" he would exclaim. (She would continue to follow)

"Don't you realize this is the *'he-man woman haters*

club'...do you know what that means!"... (She would nod affirmatively)

"Good" he replied. (She remained)

Alfalfa tries everything to make her understand, but to no avail. And by the end of the film he is hers.

The Scripture passage from Acts concerning Peter and John and the lame man healed has some similar elements. You see, Peter is trying to make the people who are standing around and watching him and John understand just what they are really doing.

Let's revisit the story. Peter and John are going to the temple. A man who is lame sitting at the gate asks for money. Peter says, "I have no silver or gold, but I give you what I have; in the name of Jesus Christ of Nazareth, walk." And he takes him by the right hand and raises him up. He was made strong and went leaping into the temple.

We are told that the people in the crowd stood around staring at Peter and John because of what has just happened.

It seems that to the people of Israel this is, in fact, something very important or at the very least interesting. It draws their attention for a little bit of time. Peter knows they are listening so he takes this opportunity to do a little preaching of his own.

Peter responds, "Men of Israel why do you stare at us as though by our own power or piety we had made him walk?" Peter is trying to show how God acts in the world and cares for people. Peter is also attempting to remind them of something else. You remember God don't you, the God that you killed, the God you denied and killed! We are witnesses to Him. And it was His Name and faith in Him that has healed this man. It is because of Jesus that we are able to do these things. The Jesus that you made to suffer and die.

What Peter is basically telling them is this, *Hey people, wake up and smell the coffee...God in Christ was here and you killed Him...But God continues to act in this world through us, and it is time that everybody realized this fact and turned again to God and asked forgiveness. If you do this, your sins are forgiven and a time of refreshing can come from the presence of the Lord!*

In other words: Hey! Will you open your eyes and realize that things are not the way you think they are? It is time for a change and this is it!

When I first read this passage it appeared to me that maybe Peter was letting them off the hook or at least giving them an opportunity to change. We know you acted in ignorance as did your rulers but what God says will happen will happen, repent therefore and turn again that your sins may be blotted out, that times of refreshing might come from the presence of the Lord. The past is done with if you only believe. And in fact, Peter is telling the crowd of people gathered that indeed they should wake up and come to Christ. Part of what is going on here is a call to act, before it is too late.

I was probably eleven years old when I first played little league baseball. Mr. Smith was my coach and our team was pretty decent. I played backup catcher and didn't get to play in many games. When I did, I didn't hit very well and my fielding was iffy at best. Dave Smith, Mr. Smith's son, was twice as big as every other kid on the team and twice as mean. He picked on me to no end. Two weeks before the end of the season an inside pitch hit my hand as I gripped the bat, broke my index finger and ended my season. To be honest, I was almost relieved.

The following year, when little league started up again, two interesting things occurred. First, I found out that I had in fact been traded to the team from the town next to us. Yes, I was the first kid in the history of little league to be traded! Mr. Smith didn't want me on his team another year. But what Mr. Smith didn't know was the second important part of the story. You see, something happened right before the season began. That's right, I got glasses!

The next season was great, our team had fun, we won a lot of games and I played so well at catcher that I was chosen to start on the all-star team at the end of the season. However, it is really the day of the all-star game that I want to share with you. Little league was a big deal in my hometown so this was a very big event. The day of the game I was as nervous as you could possibly be. I knew I had a good season, but this was the all-star game. It didn't help that Mr. Smith was the coach of the opposing team. I wanted so badly to prove something to him. I still remember the first time I went up to bat. I was so nervous I forgot to take my catchers shin guards off before I walked up to the plate...everyone laughed.

I stepped into the batter's box so worried that I would make a mistake. I watched the first pitch go right over the plate...strike one...didn't move an inch. The second...strike two...again nothing...third pitch ...strike three, you're *out*!

I walked back to the dugout and sat down and began to put my catcher's equipment back on. Right then my father came out of the stands. You need to know my father never did this, he was not one of those parents screaming and jumping up and down, he usually sat in the stands and quietly followed the game. In any event, he came down to the dugout, put his hand on my shoulder and all he said was "Mark, do me a favor, the next time you are up to bat...JUST SWING!"

Sure enough I would get one more chance to bat. It was the bottom the sixth and final inning of the game. Our team was down 4 to 2. We had two guys on base and there were two outs.

I approached the plate just as nervous as I was the first time, but I remembered what my father said...just swing! The pitcher threw the ball and I swung the bat as hard as I could and hit it to deep right center field. I rounded first and immediately headed on to second base as the outfielder retrieved the ball that had rolled to the fence. As I rounded second and began to run towards third, I looked up and who do you think was the third baseman for the other team? Dave Smith! The mean kid who outweighed me by 70 pounds! The ball was thrown in from the outfield just as I half-slid, half-slammed into Dave, knocking him over. The ball rolled up the left field line and I scrambled to my feet and ran home to score the winning run!

Why do I share that story? Because it's not so much that 'if we believe, we can do great things,' as it is 'if we believe in God, God will do great things in and through us.' In other words...JUST SWING!

See...I knew I could play, but I needed someone to remind me to swing the bat.

There is something about the scene in Acts that is worthy of note, and it concerns the crowd of people gathered about John and Peter. There is something different about the attitude and response of the crowd this time compared to when Jesus and the disciples had performed these great acts previously.

This time there is nobody present that doubts what

has happened. The scriptures tell us that they all knew the man that was healed was the same lame man that had always sat near the gate. Likewise, there is no indication on the part of the people gathered that they doubt in any way what just took place. In fact we find out a few verses later that 3000 were baptized that day in response to what had occurred.

This is important to remember because it sheds a whole new light on what Peter is saying to those gathered around him. He is not just defending the fact that he healed the man, nor is he trying to prove that this actually happened because the crowd saw it. The crowd was not there to doubt but rather they were there to believe.

He was not trying so much to convince them about Jesus Christ as he was trying to explain to them what believing in Christ could really mean to their lives.

I imagine there were two different types of responses to Peter and John that day on the way to the temple. The first one was from the people in the crowd who saw the man healed and immediately began to ask, if Peter can make the poor man walk what greater things could he do for me? Or, if a relationship to God can make this man walk, what could a relationship with God through Jesus do to make my life better?

The second group asks a similar question. If Peter and John can do these things, if I believe, like them, can I then do the great things that they do?

Peter is not surrounded by angry unbelievers so much as he is by misguided, poor intentioned believers! There is a misunderstanding on their part as to what a true relationship with Christ really means. These people are looking for rewards and benefits only, without understanding what faith, repentance and service mean. Peter says, you look at us as though we did this, as though we healed this man...we didn't...Christ and faith in Christ did!

It is not so much faith in a God that rewards us for good behavior as it is a God who forgives us for our bad actions.

There is a story about a Dr. George Harris, a former president of Amherst College. One autumn morning he rose in the chapel to address the students at the first assembly of the year. After three or four sentences he became tired. Breaking into a happy smile, he said: "I intended to give you some advice, but now I remember how much is left over from last year unused." After which he took his hat and walked out.

Perhaps Peter is looking to give some advice to the crowd. But how can he do this? After all, these are some of the same people who betrayed and killed Jesus. Maybe because he remembers that he too was unaware of just what and who Jesus was until His death on the cross and His resurrection from the dead. Peter, like the others, was ignorant as well.

E.W. Howe once said, "A good scare is worth more to a man than good advice." Perhaps there is a little of this in Peter's speech as well. Even as he reminds the crowd of what they can find in Jesus, he never lets them forget their part in His suffering and death.

How much are we today like the crowd of people gathered around John and Peter?

How often do we come to God looking for rewards for doing what we should want to do out of gratitude to Him? How often do we look at being a faithful church member as some kind of mark that says look at me, I go to church...and then we forget that to follow Christ means to serve Christ and others in God's world.

A number of years ago, a man by the name of Luigi Tarisio was found dead one morning with almost nothing in his home, nothing except 246 antique violins, which he had been collecting all his life, crammed into an attic, the best was found in the bottom of an old rickety bureau.

In his very devotion to the violin he had robbed the world of all that music all the time he treasured them. Others before him had done the very same thing, so that when the greatest of the violin collection, a Stradivarius, was first played it had previously been speechless for 147 years.

Time and again we act like Tarisio. We selfishly claim a relationship with Christ and in so doing fail to share it with others!

I remember the day our then four and three-year-old sons, John Wesley and Aaron, were sitting on the couch in our living room watching Barney the Dinosaur on TV. John had a large bowl of potato chips on his lap, Aaron wanted some and John was resisting sharing. "Daddy, if I share, I won't have any left."

"John, share with your brother."

I can still see him...in a grand gesture reaching into the bowl and pulling out a single chip and slowly giving it to Aaron. The look on Aaron's face was priceless. He might as well have put his hands on his hips and in exasperation said "Really?!"

I can't help but wonder if we aren't a bit like this when it comes to sharing our faith. Hesitant to share what we have, because we are afraid if we do so, we won't have any left?

When will we learn that the good news of Jesus Christ needs not just to be cherished, but needs to be told? All people need to hear it. And it's in the telling, in the serving, that we can find those times of refreshing that come from being in the presence of the Lord that Peter spoke of.

If we come to worship looking for power and praise for our actions, we will not find it. If we come to praise God and to empower others, and by that I mean to lift one another up, then we will find something much greater. We will find our own personal relationship with God.

There was a Garfield cartoon that showed Garfield and Odie the dog chasing one another through the yard. As Garfield heads for a tree and races up it, Odie follows him all the way up. The two of them are resting side by side when their owner John comes by. He looks up at them and says, "Odie, dogs can't climb trees." Odie immediately falls out of the tree, whereupon Garfield thinks, "It's amazing what one can accomplish when one doesn't know what one can't do."

If we are truly responding to God's call acting in our life, then we are only limited by our understanding of what it means to believe in God. John and Peter did not heal the man because of their great relationship with God. The man was healed because Peter made the man aware that HIS faith in God could make him whole.

As the people of God we have the responsibility to be like Peter and to share God's love with others. To remind others and ourselves what being a Christian is all about. We alone cannot perform miracles. We alone cannot change people's lives. But we can try to show others the One who can do these things and much more.

If we finally realize that we must play a part, no longer standing there watching three strikes go by, waiting for others to tell us we can't climb trees and then falling out. If we simply have faith in God, we too will find times of refreshing in the presence of our Lord. *Amen.*

9

EVERYBODY GO DEEP!

When I was in high school it was almost a ritual that a group of about 16 of us would gather early Saturday morning at the school, divide up into two teams and, regardless of the weather conditions, play our regular three or four hours of sandlot football. Now sandlot football, if you never played, has all the excitement of regular football, bloody noses, twisted ankles, and the frostbit fingers with none of the unnecessary trappings that complicate organized ball. You know, things like protective equipment, officials, and rules! It didn't matter if it was raining, snowing or anything else for that matter, we were always there.

Each week was pretty much like the last, several hours of playing, a few bumps and bruises, the occasional bloody nose, then we would all go home. That was until one Saturday in the late fall of 1979.

On this particular day my team wasn't doing so well. It was fourth down and about 50 yards to go. Our quarterback called us into the huddle where he proceeded to share with us the favorite call of all sandlot receivers...*EVERYBODY GO DEEP!* The ball was snapped and I began to run my pattern, which was just like everybody else's, straight down the field. He threw the ball and it was coming towards me. I jumped into the air to catch it...and then everything went black.

I later found out that as I jumped someone came from behind and knocked my legs out from under me. I flipped upside down in the air and hit the back of my head and neck on the ground. When I awoke, I found myself not only surrounded by the guys who had been playing ball, but also by a group of paramedics, who I didn't remember being there before I went down.

The paramedics were strapping me to a stretcher to transport me to the hospital. They secured me in so that I could not move and then placed me in the ambulance for the 20 minute ride to the hospital. That was one of the longest 20 minutes of my life. My head was spinning and I was dazed. But I had seen enough stories about sports injuries to know what could possibly have happened.

I was afraid. Terrified that I couldn't move my legs. So scared that I was even afraid to try and move them. But as we entered the hospital, I remember attempting to raise one leg just a little and though it was sore my leg did move. I was lucky. I came out of the whole thing with just a concussion and several days off school.

Have you ever been so uncertain about something that you felt paralyzed and unable to act or respond? That is how I felt in the ambulance that day on the way to the hospital. So afraid and uncertain that I was unwilling to even try to find out if in fact I was alright. I had a friend in college that was great at games like Trivial Pursuit. If it was an inane or useless fact you could count on him to know it. So, one weekend we entered him in a trivia challenge game on campus. He promptly proceeded to freeze up completely in front of hundreds of individuals and lose the competition. Was it that he didn't know the answers? Was he afraid to be wrong? Was he simply intimidated by the crowd? There are so many things in this life to make us fearful. Yet the response is almost always the same.

Consider the words of the Apostles' Creed:

I believe in God, the Father Almighty,
Maker of heaven and earth;
And in Jesus Christ His only Son, our Lord;
Who was conceived by the Holy Spirit,
born of the Virgin Mary,
suffered under Pontius Pilate,
was crucified, dead, and buried;*
the third day He rose from the dead;
He ascended into heaven,
and sitteth at the right hand of God the Father Almighty;
from thence He shall come to judge the quick and the dead.
I believe in the Holy Spirit,
the Holy Catholic Church,
the Communion of Saints,
the Forgiveness of Sins,
the Resurrection of the Body,
and the Life Everlasting. Amen.

I don't know if this has ever happened to you, but in my line of work it occurs frequently. When discussing Christ and Christianity with someone who does not believe or follow, I am inevitably put on the spot about any number of issues. Not the least of which are summed up in the second section of the Apostles' Creed...virgin birth...resurrection from the dead...sitting at the right hand of God...judging the living and the dead. Even the most faithful of us at one time or another has, maybe not doubted, but at least questioned to ourselves these very same statements.

And yet we often stand in church and say, "I believe this, this and this to be true." But do we?

Is it that we ourselves are paralyzed by the fear of what we might find out about our God and ourselves if we were to ask questions? After all, these combined statements have never been made concerning another single human being in all of human history.

I once had a religious studies professor in college who stated, without flinching, that not only can you not prove that Jesus was the Christ, the Messiah....but that it is also impossible to prove that Jesus of Nazareth ever really existed. A bold statement to be sure.

There is little additional source material other than the scriptures that tells us of the one called Jesus the Christ in our Holy Scriptures. Little more than footnotes in other ancient writings even acknowledge His life at all.

Did I speak out in class to argue with the professor. No. Why? Because at that point in my life, when I looked for cold hard facts to substantiate my beliefs, I could not find them.

Now before you begin to panic and wonder what this means for our relationship with God, think for a moment about what Paul wrote in his letter to the Corinthians. That *in Christ* God was reconciling the world to Himself! Do you hear that? That God was *in Christ*. That God was Christ in this world reconciling it to Himself.

Why is it so hard to look at the words of the Apostles' Creed and, as we take them apart phrase by phrase, state undeniably that we believe them to be true about the man Jesus of Nazareth that came into the world some two thousand years ago? If we were talking about a mere man, we couldn't say any of it.

Christ was fully God and fully man. And, as Christians, we freely admit that there are and always will be numerous questions that will remain unanswered about Him *in this life.* With minds as limited as our own, we cannot fully plumb the depths of the mysteries of God. What we must do, however, is to try with all that is in us to learn all we can of Him and then to follow after Him with all that we know.

I didn't have the cold hard facts to answer my professor in college, because there were no facts. What I realize now is that there is something so much greater...*faith*...when together, we repeat the words of the Apostles' Creed.

I believe in Jesus Christ, God's only Son, our Lord born of a virgin, suffered under Pontius Pilate, crucified dead and buried. On the third day He arose from the dead and ascended into heaven and sitteth at the right hand of God the Father and He shall come again to judge the quick and the dead.

When we say these words, we don't repeat them blindly, we say them as a statement of our faith. A faith that is ever changing and ever growing in its own understanding and relationship with God.

If in your mind or in your heart you question...don't be paralyzed by it. Don't be afraid to question yourself and others. Remember facts and faith are two very different things.

What we are really called to do is to use our understanding of Scripture and of things like the Apostles' Creed to help us to continue to learn more about Christ.

As the author Frank Seilhammer points out in his book, Adventure in Faith.

The wonderful thing about Jesus is that this is all that He asks us to do. He makes no more demands on us than He did on Simon Peter. "Simon, son of John, do you love me?"

He didn't ask Peter, who had been there through all the miracles, who had been a part of them himself, who had been witness to the Resurrection, who had heard Jesus preach sermon after sermon, Peter do you understand it all and can you explain it in detail to all who question?

He simply asked, do you love Me? For that is enough, if Christ has your heart then everything else is His as well.

For many of us, fear paralyzes us from serving God much of our lives. I'm afraid I might not say the right things to share Christ. I'm afraid if I give too much to the church I might not have enough left for my needs at home. I'm afraid I can't do the job the church has asked me to do, so I don't want to serve on a committee and let them down. We fear...and it's not because we lack knowledge...*we lack faith*. But we need not lack faith dear friends, for Christ's love should move us to reach out in his name.

In the town of Bath, England, on the front of Bath Abbey, are found two incredible stone carvings that depict ladders going up to heaven and down to hell. Each depicts persons climbing up to their reward, others falling off to their demise, and still others simply hanging on for dear life...unable to move up or down.

Fear freezes some in their tracks and ultimately they too will fall. How many people do you know like that right now? Just clinging *onto*, but not really *growing* in faith?

Not completely turning their backs on God, but just unsure what to do or where to turn next? You can help them, believe it or not. We, in fact, have an opportunity to reach people and save lives.

In the first church I served, in the city of Pittsburgh, my office was located next to the room in which the choir practiced prior to the church service on Sunday mornings. Normally this room was quiet during the week. However, I remember one cold winter afternoon, while I was sitting at my desk trying to complete a bunch of paperwork and letters, I heard the piano tuner arrive and enter the room next door to tune the piano for the choir.

I could not help but listen as he repetitively would pound one key, time and time again, to bring it into tune. He would then move to the next key, and once again strike it time after time until it was perfect.

This process went on and on for some time, and though it seemed quite repetitive, I knew it had a purpose. He continued his way up the keyboard. When he had finished, when he had accomplished his goal, he took a moment to enjoy the fruits of his labor. He played a very short, but absolutely beautiful, few measures of Pachelbel's Canon. The music filled the hallway and I stopped completely so that I might not miss a note. Then, as quickly as it began, it was over. The hallway grew silent once more.

I remember thinking to myself, *no one else would hear him play that day, so no one would know that he was even there*. How frustrating it must be not to be appreciated, acknowledged, or even heard.

But then I realized it wasn't over. For not only had I heard the music he played, and it had left an impression on me, but he had tuned an instrument that would then be used to assist the choir and children's choirs of that church as they prepared each week to share their gift of music with the congregation and God.

For centuries now we have been listening to and rejoicing in the music of the One who came into the world to tune our souls. And though few recognized His presence at the time, and while still even today others refuse to acknowledge He was ever here, the music continues to ring forth.

We too are instruments that can make beautiful music as we share Christ's love!

We live in a broken world. Yes, the news is often bleak and divisive. But people have not stopped believing, in fact, perhaps now more than ever in this country, people are deciding that *just clinging to the ladder* isn't enough. It's time to be moving upward and I believe people are seeking something to believe in. This is a wonderful opportunity to share who and what we are with the world. If you love God, and you love your neighbor...*share your love of God with your neighbor!*

If anyone is *in Christ*, He is a new creation, the old has gone, the new has come. Thank God that we have been made new. And, having been made new, fear not! Let us go into the world *with faith filled love*, and *share Christ! Amen.*

10

BETTER THAN I KNOW MYSELF

SUGGESTED READING: JOHN 4:1-42

It was my junior year of high school; I had recently obtained my driver's license and my father was finally allowing me to take the family car out by myself. On the evening in question I was on my way to an *Interact* meeting. *Interact* was a service organization, connected with Rotary, that did projects in the community (lest you think my motives as a teen to be completely altruistic, I, in fact, joined the club because the girl I liked was a member).

This particular evening I arrived a few minutes early and quickly jumped from my father's Plymouth Valiant to go into the meeting, when I realized that I had left my keys in the car. Fortunately, I noticed that I hadn't locked the door so I was going to easily retrieve them and head into the meeting.

The problem was, however, that the door was somehow jammed shut. I pulled and pulled, all the while wondering what could possibly be keeping it closed. There must be something stuck in the door I thought. So I bent over to look closely through the window while continually pulling, now frantically, at the driver's side front door.

Remember the old Warner Brothers Roadrunner cartoons, where Wile E. Coyote is chasing after the Road Runner, and inevitably finds himself running off a cliff or standing under a falling anvil? At first, he fails to realize the danger he is in, and then right before the crash there is this brief second of recognition of what is about to happen, but by then it is too late, and there is nothing he can do but suffer the consequences?

Well, in the next fraction of a second I realized just how stupid it was for me to be leaning forward and pulling backward at the same time...but it was too late! The door sprung open, the corner of it *smashing* me right between the eyes!

I immediately thought of the new glasses my parents had just bought me and nothing else. My head hurt, but if I broke my glasses my parents would kill me. I grabbed them off of my face to see if they were OK! *Amazingly* they were unscratched!

As I held them in my hands looking at them thinking how fortunate I was that they were not broken, feeling somewhat relieved but realizing more and more that my head *really* hurt! I noticed blood start to drip into my hands and onto my glasses.

While the door had somehow missed my glasses altogether, it did manage to put a V-shaped hole right in the center of my forehead!

I sat through the meeting with a towel on my head and afterwards went back to my then girlfriend Karen's house where she and her mother attempted to stop the bleeding.

I remember Karen's words, "Mark, you better go to the emergency room and have them put a stitch in it for you."

I was in no position to argue, the pain was getting worse and worse, my head was throbbing. So my mother drove me to the hospital emergency room where we waited for several more hours. Time dragged on forever, but I was at least thankful that finally I would get some relief from the pain. After all, doctors are supposed to be compassionate and caring individuals are they not?

I was eventually escorted to an examination room, where I was made to lie on the table, and the doctor came in. He took one look at me, as he picked up his needle and thread, and this *caring, compassionate doctor* said, "This is going to hurt *a lot*!" and then he began to stitch. I will never forget this as long as I live!

Well, a great deal of pain *and 12 stitches*, not *one*, but *twelve stitches later* I was on my way home, and actually quite rapidly the pain began to lessen. And I know I healed much faster than if I had taken care of it myself.

Everyone at one time or another in life has experienced pain. Perhaps it was physical pain, maybe emotional or even spiritual. Perhaps it was the pain of the loss of a loved one or the pain of feeling lost and alone. Some of us even now carry with us our own private pain that we and we alone believer we must bear.

The fact that we as humans experience pain, and quite often at that, is nothing new. The Gospel of John tells us of an individual who carries with her person some heavy baggage, so to speak. And with that baggage most certainly must have come pain.

Jesus is on His way from Judea back home to Galilee. In order to make such a journey He and His disciples had to pass through Samaria. The Samaritans and Jews did not think very highly of one another. In fact you might say they hated each other. Among their differences was the fact that the Jews believed one must go to Jerusalem to worship God while the Samaritans thought it possible to worship Yahweh in their own land.

It was commonly understood that the Jew believed himself to be superior to the Samaritan in many ways. That is why this particular event in Jesus's ministry is so significant. It shows Him reaching out to others, beyond the immediate circle of the Jews, to those deemed less important or less worthy by Jewish society. And so begins a rather surprising chain of events. A Samaritan woman draws water at a well. Jesus, a Jew, approaches her. Not only is it unusual that a Jew would approach a Samaritan, but a man would never talk to a woman in broad daylight. *Then* He asks her to give Him something to drink. This woman must have felt as though someone had hit her over the head. Perhaps stunned and a bit confused.

During the course of their conversation, Jesus shares with her that He can offer *her* something...*living water!* She does not understand, but she is curious. The conversation continues and she begins to feel more comfortable and at ease. Just then, Jesus, like my emergency room doctor, says in so many words, "This is going to hurt a lot!" For it is at this point that Jesus tells her to get her husband. He knows she's had five and lives with yet another. What He is saying, in essence, is, *I know you, I know your past, all of it, and I know what you're doing now!* Stitch by stitch He makes His point. Just think how you would feel if someone came to you and began to tell you things about yourself that no one else knew. You would likely feel at a disadvantage, humbled, overwhelmed, and afraid.

This Samaritan woman is little different. How painful it must be to hear about herself. Then again, how painful was it to be carrying around a burdened and heavy heart?

Many scholars believe that the next portion of this story is included in John's Gospel to lift up and deal with the issue of where and how God is to be worshipped, and it does in fact do that. But I believe there is also a much more basic explanation for the Samaritan woman's comments.

I think an argument can be made that she is merely attempting to change the subject. Jesus starts telling her about her past and she admits it's true, but then attempts to turn the conversation. "My people say we should worship God here and You say Jerusalem," she might as well be saying, "How about that weather we're having, huh Jesus?"

Haven't you ever tried the same tactic when someone began telling you something you didn't want to hear?

When one of our sons was very young and would need to be reprimanded for something he had done, he would receive a *time out.* Inevitably, as soon as he would take his seat in the "time out" chair, he would begin to shout, "I have to use the potty!" We learn quite early to attempt to escape discomforting situations with all kinds of excuses.

Yes, once this Samaritan woman realizes Jesus knows all about her, and that in fact she cannot hide anything from Him, her initial embarrassment and discomfort ultimately lead to acceptance and relief and even a sense of excitement.

It's as if, the stitching is done, with relief soon following. And the excitement comes in the form of going and sharing her good news that she has found the Messiah with others. In turn her witness changes not only her life, but the lives of many Samaritans from that city that believed in Him because of her testimony.

Can you imagine coming face to face with One who knows you better than you know yourself? One who knows even the deepest darkest secrets of your life? Does the prospect of such an encounter fill you with joy or a sense of dread?

For many the prospect of such an encounter would be terrifying. Despite how open and honest we each claim to be, we also know there are private parts to our lives that we keep hidden away from everyone else. But remember what happened to the Samaritan woman, once she realized that there was really nothing that she *could hide* from Jesus. All of the sudden her pain went away. *What pain is that*, you ask? The pain we all keep inside at times, the pain of everyday life, the pain of not having any real direction in our lives, the pain that we seldom express to anyone, even those closest to us. A pain that can only be taken away by a GOD of love, when we realize that God is there for us.

Notice, the woman did not seek Jesus out in order for her life to be changed. In much the same way humanity did not seek out Christ that we might be changed. In both cases God enters into people's lives, in spite of humanity's response, and because of God's love for us, offers us a new chance, a new start, a new life.

Because this woman allows herself to remain open to the living water that is Jesus, her life continues to be transformed and renewed in the days that follow, and her life in turn becomes a witness to change still others.

The scriptures tell us that *we have this treasure in earthen vessels, so that the power of God may be made known through us.* We are all human beings, and as such we are imperfect and, dare I say it, *sinful.* We are chipped, cracked and broken vessels. The fact is that none of us are without flaws, cracks and holes. As someone once said, the only way to keep a broken vessel full is by *keeping the faucet turned on!* It is up to each of us as Christians to keep the water turned on.

Christ offers us living water that changes our life. But it is not just a sip that we take today and forget or still thirst for tomorrow. It is an ever flowing water that can fill us over and over again. The living water that is Christ is not the few drops from a faucet, rather it is like a waterfall that pours over us and into us over and over again. And if we allow it and if we open ourselves to it, we are transformed and ultimately are enabled to help transform others.

How many people in pain are there in the world today? I wonder. As we continue our journey through this life, let us not forget that there is One who indeed knows us better than we know ourselves. One who loves us, and desires to see our lives transformed.

There is One who has come into the world, to confront us in our sin, not to condemn but to forgive. Let Christ enter, flow into, flood over your life again this day and give thanks that He knows you better than you know yourself and that He loves you. Then go out into God's world and be a witness to others of that love. *Amen.*

11

COME TO THE BANQUET

SUGGESTED READING: LUKE 14:16-24

J esus tells the story of a very wealthy man who prepares an incredible feast for his invited guests. However, something very unusual happens when it is time for the feast to begin. At a time when all should be excited and anxious to attend the banquet, each in turn declines and tells him that for one reason or another, they cannot come.

*A party with no guests, i*s not much of a party. So the master sends his servants into the streets to invite all those individuals whom you would normally not expect to find at such an event. Once this is done He sends them out yet another time to search farther and wider to invite all who wish to attend. It is only then that the banquet can begin. A time of celebration, a time of fellowship, a time of joy and togetherness.

What must be going through the mind of those individuals who actually accepted the invitation to attend the banquet? Consider that these are not your typical dinner guests that end up gathering at the table in this man's home, are they? Many are wondering, *why are we here in the first place?* We don't belong in a home like this, we don't even know how to behave in such situations. This is a dinner party at the home of the wealthiest man in town, I hope I don't embarrass myself!

My senior year of high school, I had the opportunity to participate in a music festival in Philadelphia. As part of the preparation for the event, students from all over Pennsylvania traveled to a suburb of Philadelphia and practiced for the better part of a week for a concert on Saturday.

In the evenings we were to be housed by families from the community. The night we arrived, we discovered that four of us would be staying with one particularly wealthy family. They picked us up at the school and drove us home to what could only be described as a *mansion* in an elite section of the city.

They helped us to our individual rooms and informed us that dinner would be served at eight that evening. I remember thinking that this wasn't at all like what I was used to at home. I hoped I wouldn't do anything to embarrass myself. Dinnertime arrived and we made our way to the largest dining room I have ever seen that wasn't connected to a Sheraton or Ramada Inn.

The table was covered with beautiful china and more silver than I had ever seen. I made my way to my chair and noticed something that made me very nervous.

Understand that I grew up in a family where we sat at the table with one knife, one fork and one spoon per place setting. Surrounding my plate, on this particular table, was more silverware than my entire family would use at a single meal! Four different forks, three spoons, at least two knives and a couple utensils that I didn't even recognize! *Which one do I use for what?* Do I start on the inside and work my way out, or the outside and work my way in. Everyone else appeared to know what they were doing so I couldn't ask. I would just pray that everything went OK.

In fact, everything was fine during the soup and salad, but when we came to the main course of steak...it happened. The conversation went back and forth, around the table. We shared about our families and our schools. We expressed our excitement about the upcoming concert and we all continued to eat.

As I took my silver fork in hand and stuck it into the steak to cut it with my knife, I must have pushed too hard because just then the fork bent in half and my hand pushed right into the steak. I honestly can't tell you if anyone noticed or not, though I suspect they all did. The next ten minutes, or what seemed like an eternity, were a blur. I quickly grabbed the fork and brought it down under the table as I tried to unbend it without snapping it in two! The conversation continued and I sat there smiling and sweating bullets trying to bend it back into some presentable form.

The next day my host took me aside and informed me that she had seen it all but assured me that it was OK.

There were many at the banquet in Luke's Gospel account who were unsure what to do as well, until their host made them feel at ease and at home. What about the other guests? What were they really like and what were their needs? How would attending such a feast benefit any of them?

Let me share with you briefly the stories of a few special individuals who attended banquets of their own:

Mary was a woman who lived on the streets of the city. But Mary knew what she believed. Every Sunday she would come to church, normally ten minutes late, and walk right up the center aisle and sit in the very first pew. It was common for her to begin putting curlers in her hair during her time in worship. She always made herself at home, oftentimes stretching out across the entire pew with her legs up, in order to relax. But the thing I remember most about Mary is that as soon as the sermon began, she listened intently, and if she didn't feel you were preaching the truth, she just stood up and walked right back out. She always returned the following week, but on many, many occasions, she too would stay to be a part of the banquet.

William, had a speech impediment and a learning disorder. He too, lived on the streets of downtown Pittsburgh. William was always down on his luck, and in addition to everything else was an alcoholic. It was a Maundy Thursday Communion service at the church. The minister stood to give the scripture lesson and then her message. "The Gospel lesson comes from.....", she then proceeded to begin her sermon.

"Excuse me, excuse me" a somewhat slurred voice came shouting from the third pew from the front, interrupting the sermon. "What page is the Bible reading on Ma'am? I can't seem to find it." Another minister made his way to William and helped him find the page and they sat there together during the meditation. It was then time for Communion. Being Maundy Thursday, a table had been prepared at the front of the sanctuary where the people sat to receive the elements. As William came forward at sat at the table he began to weep and ask Jesus for help in his life. He was afraid to drink the grape juice used for the Holy Communion because he thought it was wine. We stood with him and prayed with him that night as he attended the banquet.

These individuals were invited and attended the banquet. Not your typical guests for a party or celebration, but the guests that Jesus tells us were there.

And lest we presume that we have little in common with them, think on these things.

Has there ever been a time in your life when you felt little need for God or religion and something like music or a sermon or someone like a friend or family member spoke to you? Come to the banquet.

Have there been times when you came to God and His church with your mind made up, and not really listening closely for God speaking through others? You can still join Mary at the banquet.

Do you come to God with questions as to why things happen the way they do in your life, are you asking for help, are you looking for answers? Join William at the banquet.

Who are the poor, the crippled the blind the lame and the outcasts? *We all are*...and the banquet is ready.

It is time that each of us realizes that the invitation has been given to be a part of God's glorious banquet. The thing is, none of us know for certain when that eternal banquet will begin. When is our last day of life on this earth? When might the Lord return to claim His own? No one knows but God himself. What we can be certain of, is that an invitation to an event is only good until that event begins. Once the party or banquet is over, invitations are of no further value.

How many have paused, if only for a moment during the events of recent years and wondered, are these signs of something? Is God trying to get our attention? Is the end near? The only legitimate answer to that question is...*I don't know*. When Jesus walked the earth, He said that even He didn't know, the angels in heaven didn't know, *only* God the Father knew.

Why is it, that we are quick to think such things, even for a fleeting moment, but still continue to live lives that are not centered on God, not dedicated to His service, and not focused on sharing His love. In other words, if we really believe God is trying to get our attention, attempting to get us to act differently, say something or do something in a way we have not done before, why are we not responding to Him and allowing Him to transform our lives?

The host of this heavenly banquet seeks to make all feel at home. The invitation is there for the taking. *Now*. But if we will not respond to it, the banquet will still go on, only we will be absent from it. I don't know about you, but this is a party I really do not want to miss.

PART II DISCUSSION QUESTIONS

1. What is your earliest recollection as a child?
2. Was/is the church a place you found/find comfort and support?
3. Have you ever felt lost? How was it that you were ultimately able to find your way again?
4. Are you comfortable sharing your faith? If not, what is it that holds you back?
5. Does the idea that God desires to be intimately involved in your life bring you peace or anxiety?

PART III

LESSONS FROM LIFE

Isn't it interesting that so much of our faith development occurs outside the walls of the church and the home? Life with our friends, at school and work present numerous challenges and blessings. And yet, as we reflect upon how we deal with such moments we often see that we grow not only closer to our friends but also to our God.

12

EXCESS BAGGAGE

SUGGESTED READING: I JOHN 1:5-10

It was the first term of my first year of college. I felt it was time to spend a weekend at home with my family and see my then girlfriend, and future wife, Karen. After all, I had been at school for two whole weeks by that point and I deserved a break from the rigors of the academic world. I loaded my suitcase with several pairs of jeans, three or four shirts, my sneakers and dress shoes, a suit, in case I needed it, a jacket, some other dirty laundry for my mother to wash, and because I knew that I would be spending so much time at home I packed what must have been every book from every class I was taking that term as well.

The combined weight of the now two suitcases I had packed was well over fifty pounds. I left the school at about three in the afternoon on Friday afternoon walked the two miles down the hill to the Greyhound Bus Station by 4:30, took a two hour bus to Pittsburgh, waited in the Pittsburgh bus station another two hours for my bus then rode for another two plus hours and arrived in Altoona sometime around 11 o'clock in the evening. Then Sunday morning I would begin the whole process in reverse. Bus to Pittsburgh, then a wait, bus to Meadville then a long walk this time up the hill two miles to the school. If I remember correctly the round trip cost me something in the area of 60 dollars. My total number of hours at home totaled about 36.

What I remember most about that trip however, was my return to school. More specifically, my walk up the hill on that hot September afternoon to the school, carrying all those essentials that I had chosen to take with me on my trip in the first place. I was about a quarter of the way up the hill when I asked myself, *why did I take three different pairs of pants, four shirts and a suit? Did I really plan on wearing them?* Especially when I realized I was wearing the same sweat shirt and pair of jeans walking up the hill on Sunday that I had been wearing as I walked down the hill on Friday.

As I approached the three quarter point, by this time dragging one bag with the other slung over my back, I thought *just how many of the seven or eight books that I had packed ever even came out of the suitcase? Not a one, and some of them ended up staying in the bag most of the term.* I, in fact had been carrying around a great deal of excess baggage with me that weekend and once I realized it, it never happened again.

It occurs to me that anytime we take a trip, more often than not we take a lot of things with us that we do not really need. Or, at the very least, we often find out, after the fact, that we have taken with us much more than we needed. One thing is for certain and that is that excess baggage serves no purpose other than to take up room, weigh us down, and believe me...slow us down on our journey!

We all carry a lot of excess baggage with us on this journey of life. Things that slow us down, that take up space in our hearts and minds and that keep us from continuing on the journey that God has provided for us. The baggage I speak of is guilt, anger, envy, pride, disappointment, self-pity, jealousy, hatred, resentment, fear of failure, and bitterness. These are the things that, as John says in his letter, keep us living in darkness. All this baggage I have listed has one thing in common. In weighing us down it serves to keep us from being in community and fellowship with others. John uses the images of light and darkness and equates them with right and wrong, life and death.

There is one thing about light that we should remember. It *always* overcomes darkness! A light or lamp can illuminate a dark room but even the darkest of nights cannot swallow up a light that shines into it. The darkness of which John spoke has another word that we, all too often anymore, do not like to hear...*sin*. It's a word we have become very uncomfortable using to describe actions, particularly our own. We recognize that evil exists in the world, and we are also willing to admit that we are not perfect, but we still have a difficult time admitting that indeed *sin* affects us in some way or another.

But, as John says in Scripture *"If we claim to be sinless we are deceiving ourselves, and the truth has no place in us"*. The fact is that we all fall short of the mark at times. We know, others know, God knows it, but as verse 9 tells us *"If we acknowledge our sins, God is faithful and righteous, so that God will forgive our sins and purify us from every kind of unrighteousness."*

How important it is to recognize the fact that we all fall short and yet, through the love of God are forgiven. It all seems so easy, doesn't it? Just like that our sins, our wrongs, our mistakes are forgotten. But it wasn't easy. The cost for such a task was great, even unthinkable, and this we would do well to remember. The cost was the cross. It took a God, Who loves the world so much that He was willing to send His Son into that world and allow Him to be crucified and die on a cross in order to make a very uncaring and unforgiving world understand that in fact it was forgiven. Even when we realize the unthinkable limits to which our God was willing to go to forgive an unforgivable world, there is still some excess baggage that we as human beings carry with us.

John realized it and wrote of it in verse 7 "If we live in the light as He (God) Himself is in the light, then we share fellowship with each other, and the blood of Jesus, God's Son, purifies us from every sin."

If sin is darkness, leading a good life is light. Therefore if we are in the light we are in fellowship with others and if we are in fellowship with others we are in the light. One feeds off of the other. When we are truly in fellowship with others we are being the people that God wants us to be by living in the light. It is impossible to be a Christian, not just a good Christian, but a Christian by yourself. We are only Christians when we are sharing with and caring for others. Even though we are people who are forgiven by God we sometimes have difficulty forgiving others, and worse yet, we have difficulty forgiving ourselves.

I have a somewhat unique nickname for my daughter Annie. I call her "Trouble."

When Annie was about a year and a half to two years old her mother had given her a bath and put her pajamas on to go to bed. We laid her in her crib and turned out the lights. A few moments later we heard a splash, walked into the bathroom and found Annie; still fully dressed in her pajamas sitting in the middle of the bathtub laughing and splashing away. We lifted her out and sternly told her she was in trouble. We dried her off and sent her back to bed.

A few days later, I was home alone with Annie while her mother was at the store. At one point I realized Annie had disappeared and I went to find her. Of course she was back in the bathroom. Only this time she had managed to take all of her plastic tub toys and load them into the commode. It was literally filled to the top with plastic ducks and boats, etc. At first, I was going to leave the toys in place to show her mother just what Annie had done while she was gone. But something told me that I better not. Instead, I began to retrieve one toy at a time, only to find at the very bottom, covered by several inches of water... my wallet! As I pulled it out of the commode, I turned and looked at my *now smiling daughter*, sitting in the middle of the bathroom floor who clearly said to her *not too pleased father*..."I'm trouble!"

It occurs to me that many times in this life, we know we have fallen short. We know we have made mistakes. We know we are "in trouble." And we feel as though that is the way it must remain. Nothing can change it. The excess baggage of life simply weighs us down and from this point on our first, middle and last name is "trouble." But it needn't be. In Christ our lives can change!

A woman with a suitcase in hand was late for her train. She frantically dashed through the station to the tracks as the train was just beginning to pull out. Just as the train began to move, she was able to jump quickly aboard. Even after she was safely on the train for some time she was breathing very heavy, shaking a bit and still clutching her suitcase. Just then the conductor said to her, "You can put your suitcase down now, the train will carry it from here." *Amen.*

13

HELP WANTED

SUGGESTED READING: JOSHUA 3:7-17

Wanted: effective, efficient, energetic worker, willing and able to take orders, delegate responsibilities and communicate effectively with subordinates. Must be able to show restraint in developing new program ideas and demonstrate sound judgment in implementing said programs. Previous experience in this line of work is helpful but not absolutely necessary...and one added footnote....you will be succeeding a most beloved, and sometimes feared, leader who has led the organization for many, many years.

Such was the job description that Joshua had to deal with as he began his leadership of the children of Israel after the death of Moses. Most would agree that Joshua had his hands full in trying to fill the shoes of Moses and that very few people in their right mind would want such a job in the first place. Yet without a doubt Joshua proves to be absolutely the right man for the job.

As this scripture lesson indicates, even from the very beginning of Joshua's tenure as leader of the Israelites, we see someone quite able to live up to everything desired in his job description.

In order to see just how fine a job Joshua is doing, I thought it might be helpful to compare him to two people I have encountered over the course of my life who also were hired under similar circumstances.

Remember the job qualifications:

Wanted: effective, efficient, energetic worker, willing and able to take orders, delegate responsibilities, and communicate effectively with subordinates. Must be able to show restraint in developing new program ideas and demonstrate sound judgment in implementing said programs. Previous experience in this line of work is helpful but not absolutely necessary...and one added footnote...you will be succeeding a most beloved and sometimes feared leader who has led the organization for many, many years.

This time, however, the job wasn't as leader of the Israelites, it was for registrar at a small liberal arts college.

It was my senior year at college, and I was fortunate enough to find a part time job working in the registrar's office at the school. This was the office that kept track of everybody's grades and transcripts, as well as organized the class schedule for each term. The office staff consisted of two secretaries, two part-time students and the registrar herself, Sally Anderson, a kindly but tough matronly woman who liked to brag she had been registrar at the college since before the big war.

Nobody knew for sure whether she meant World War II or the Civil War, nevertheless she had obviously been there longer than most people at the school had been alive. It seemed evident that the methods used in 1980 had changed very little since 1880. While computers were beginning to be used to speed the process, the general tasks involved in record keeping remained unchanged. And everything ran smooth as silk.

Part way through the year, Sally announced that she would be retiring and that the college had already found an assistant to come on board for the reminder of that year to become acquainted with the job. The plan being that the assistant would then take over the job the following year.

Into our idyllic office, where everyone got along, was introduced Ms. Lucy Smith, United States Army, retired. And while I am not sure what her responsibilities were in the military, I suspect she must have been a boot camp instructor. She entered our lives like a tornado. She suggested changing the way files were kept, time cards were punched, classes were chosen, and all of this while the real registrar was still in our midst. She was loud, insensitive, and listened to no one. I still remember one intense conversation Sally had with her. It was simply, "there is a reason we haven't changed the filing system in years...IT WORKS!" And believe it or not, the following fall when Sally retired, Lucy was also asked to move on as well.

Efficient? Perhaps. Energetic? Certainly. Delegating responsibilities? Absolutely! But able to take orders? NO! Able to communicate with subordinates? Not at all. Demonstrating sound judgment in implementing programs? Not once. Effective? *Never*!

A second example of not exactly living up to the job expectations, took place in a local congregation I served as an associate minister while in seminary. Of course in this case, a beloved minister of many years moved on to another church and a new minister was hired to lead the church.

This gentleman was always worried about doing everything *just so*. I will never forget the week we held the first Communion service after his arrival. There were three ministers on staff that would be assisting with Communion. We were all called into his office together at which time he actually pulled out a diagram of the sanctuary with the Communion table highlighted and three circles on one side. At first I thought he was joking, just to break the ice with staff, then he pulled out a pointer and I knew he was actually serious.

"Mark, this is you on the left. Gail, this is you on the right and here I am, right in the center. The microphone will be six inches back from the table. We will stand two feet apart. When I give the blessing over the elements, Mark will proceed to his right to distribute. Gail, go to your left, meet in the middle, then as you return to the table we will each rotate one place to the right. Gail will bless the cup and Mark and I will distribute. Left, right, meet in the middle, rotate for final prayer. *Does everybody know what they're doing?*" It felt more life we were breaking the huddle for the second half of the big game than it did we were preparing for the Lord's Supper!

Of course we just sat there staring at what he had done. We had all helped with Communion so many times and the area in which we served was so open that it had never even been an issue as to where one person needed to be. Everything took care of itself. But he had a plan. He wanted to make it work *his way*. That Sunday as Communion began, the prayers were offered and then he picked up the tray of cups and began to distribute them before we had first blessed and passed the bread. When he realized what he had done, he became even more flustered and even though the congregation was very understanding and not a single concern was ever mentioned on their part, he constantly *for months* would talk about how he had messed up the service. Colleagues and coworkers tried to give encouragement and make suggestions to help him but he would not listen. This was the first of many such overreactions to missteps those first few months of his ministry. It was no surprise to many that he soon left that position.

Here again was someone willing and energetic, but really unprepared and ineffective when it came to doing the job. And the reality of all of this is that oftentimes the wrong person is chosen for the job in every area of life, and they do fail. However, just as many times the right person is found for a position and they do quite well.

What is the difference between an effective leader and an ineffective one? To answer that let us return to the story of Joshua.

Joshua is preparing the people to finally enter into Canaan. They have been through much since they left Egypt. They have endured trials with God's help, they have made mistakes to be sure, but they have repented. They are ready for a strong leader to bring them home.

This is Joshua's big chance. God tells Joshua *it is time, take the Ark of the Covenant, have the priests step into the water, the waters will part, the people will pass through.*

Here is the first real indication that Joshua is able to take orders. To clarify this, we need to have an understanding of the lay of the land. The Sea of Galilee is to the north, the Dead Sea is but a few miles to the south of where the Israelites are, and yet God tells Joshua to cross the Jordan here at Gilgal. Even though the account from scripture mentions that the banks of the Jordan are overflowing because of the time of year, even at its widest, the Jordan is little more than a glorified creek.

Now if I were in Joshua's place, I would be thinking, *gee, the people still remember Moses dividing the Red Sea and allowing them to pass through and here I am at this bend of the Jordan, holding back a mighty trickle of water for them to cross, surely this is going to look awfully unimpressive to them.*

Why doesn't Joshua say, *"Hey God, why don't we go a little further north and you can part the Sea of Galilee or a little further south and we will pass through the Dead Sea? These would be much more impressive and noteworthy! The people will certainly listen to me after that, don't you think?"*

No indication is given that Joshua questions God even for a moment. He simply obeys his God and instructs the priests and the people to pass through.

Unlike Moses, Joshua is in need of the help of others to make the waters stop, for it is nothing he says, but rather when the feet of the priests carrying the Ark of the Covenant touch the waters that they cease to flow.

Truly, Joshua leads by being a faithful follower first, and an effective communicator with his subordinates and coworkers second.

Because Joshua obeys his God and crosses the Jordan where he does, the people of Israel are in perfect position to begin to reclaim their homeland. Jericho is but a few miles away from Gilgal. With little energy spent in crossing the Jordan, Joshua and his people would soon be ready to fight that battle and watch the walls come tumbling down. Joshua's faithful obedience to God's instructions would ultimately prove him an extremely effective leader of his people.

Now ask yourself, how effective are you as leader? No,

not necessarily a leader at work or at school, or even at home or church for that matter. I mean, *how effective are you in being a leader for Christ? You* see, being called as a *leader for Christ,* doesn't necessarily mean being called to part the Red Sea, or the Jordan River, or to raise the dead, or even to preach the Word to a congregation on Sunday mornings.

What we often forget is that God's requests of us are not always to move mountains or have all knowledge, or to speak in tongues. More often we are simply called to have love in our hearts and to share love in our lives.

Faithful followers *of* Christ make faithful leaders *to* Christ. God is speaking to each of us, not telling us that we need to part the Red Sea, but rather, God is simply calling us to share His love with one another and the world.

14

LET DOWN YOUR NETS: TRUST

It was the final week of my senior year of college. Graduation would be in just three more days. The next day parents and family would start arriving for Baccalaureate and other services. Soon our time as college students would come to a close.

My housemate George and I sat on the front porch of our house on the edge of campus, talking through the night about things that we had done and not done. As we recounted many of our adventures during the previous four years, we continued to stare at the shadow of the Campus Center Auditorium that stood in the distance, two blocks from our front porch. The Campus Center was the largest building on campus, one story high in some sections and as high as five stories at others.

As we stared at the Campus Center, suddenly we could make out the silhouette of a man walking across the very top of the building. We immediately knew it had to be our friend Allan. You see, Allan was rather eccentric. A computer specialist, who "marched to a different drummer" than most people. Allan was constantly getting himself in trouble with the administration for doing things like using his rock climbing gear to scale the library in his boxer shorts. We thought perhaps we better go and see if he was alright and try to keep him out of further trouble. It was now four in the morning, as we went on our search to find Allan and get him down.

We walked to the building, but nothing was open. How did he get up on the roof if all the doors were locked? We walked around the building and discovered a wooden desk chair propped up against a brick wall. And so began our adventure. We decided to try our best to scale the building as Allan must have. We had no gear, no ropes, nothing! What followed might be hard for you to picture, but please try because I promise you it's true.

From where we were standing at the side of the building it was approximately 25 feet to the first roof landing. But the only thing to grasp onto was a light fixture that stuck out from the brick wall about 12 feet up. It seemed impossible but we were willing to try it anyway. This is what we did: George took the chair and put it against the brick wall. I held it in place as he balanced himself first on the back of the chair, then on my shoulders long enough to grab the metal bar above the light.

From there he pulled himself up to stand on that metal bar about 12 feet up. Once there, he reached down and pulled me up with him. Now the two of us are standing on this metal rod sticking out of the wall, still having to go another 12 or 13 feet with absolutely nothing to grab onto. We decided that I would climb up George's back and stand on his shoulders, grab the edge of the roof and then George would climb up over me. Sounds simple doesn't it? After much effort, sweat and tears, I found myself balanced on George's back. Now I am literally about 17 or 18 feet in the air and I could not quite touch the edge of the roof. I was ready to give up when George said he would lift me by my feet! As I stretched out to grab the edge of the roof, I heard a thump, a swish and then a thud. I held onto the roof for dear life and managed to pull myself up, and I turned to look down to see George had fallen to the ground below. He was lying face down and unconscious on the cement.

Well, needless to say at this point I became very concerned and being the compassionate guy that I am, all I could think about was *not whether or not George was alive*, but rather, *how am I going to get down off this building!?*

It was almost at this exact moment that I noticed Allan walking along the side of the road on his way back to his house, no worse for wear and seemingly oblivious to the world.

Realizing that the sun would soon be up and that campus security would probably not understand our urgent need to scale the building in the fashion we had chosen, I began to quickly survey my options of how I was going to get off the building. I had none! Every place I turned was even higher than the one before. So I returned to where George was laying on the ground and began yelling at him to get up. After a few minutes he began to stir. The sun was beginning to rise and I just wanted this all to be over with so I was willing to try anything. When George said, *"if you jump I will catch you,"* at that moment, it didn't sound as crazy as it might to you.

Have you ever played that game where someone drops a dollar bill between your two fingers and you try to catch it by quickly squeezing your fingers together? This tests your reflexes I suppose. Well this was the same principle. George said if I would jump he would try to pin me against the building on the way down so I wouldn't break my legs. So, I jumped and George pushed and somehow I landed without breaking any bones, but perhaps an inch or two shorter, and we both limped back to the house.

Years later I performed the wedding ceremony for another of our roommates in New York and we all sat and reminisced about our college days and I told them that I have always referred to that as my *leap of faith* story. Doing something, not just because someone asked me to, but also *because I had no other option*! Luke Chapter 5 presents us with a very similar situation.

While many of the stories of scripture appear in two, three, or even four of the gospel accounts, this is one of the passages that appears only once. Does this account of the calling of Peter, James and John lie in contrast to the other accounts, where Jesus comes to Andrew and Peter in the boat, or the account of Andrew bringing Peter to Christ? Not necessarily, in fact I believe this story complements the others.

From the setting of the story it seems obvious that Peter and the others know who Jesus is when He comes to them inquiring about their catch during the night. They are very dismayed because they have caught nothing. So Jesus tells them to try one more time, but this time in the deep waters (the more difficult areas to fish). In no time at all the catch is breaking their net because of its size.

You see, Peter didn't do this just because Jesus told him to, he did it because *he had no other option...nothing they had tried to that point had worked*. So why not? They cast their nets and they were rewarded with an incredible catch. Why do you go to church? Why do you pray? Is it that these are the best ways for you to express your relationship to your God? Or is it that nothing else has given you direction in your life? Are you really looking for something in particular in your relationship with Jesus Christ?

If so, what is it? Is it wealth, fame, comfort, happiness, love? What kind of net have you cast in order to try and receive that gift?

I find it amazing how many people pray for God to take care of them and then just sit on their backsides and do nothing for themselves. Or those that say they pray for their church and yet do not do anything to support its ministries, either financially or with their time. There are those who want to be loved and yet find it impossible to show kindness and caring unconditionally to others. And yet it is our ability as human beings to show love, to work and to give of ourselves to others. These things, in a very real sense are our *nets* that we can cast into the world, in hopes of making our catch.

Yet sometimes, no matter how hard we try, no matter how much love we try to show to others, it is not returned. No matter how much time we give to a project in the church, it does not succeed. Or no matter how much money we give to a ministry, it continues to be ineffective. Then there are those personal relationships with family or others that you work at and work at, with patience and understanding, and little or nothing ever seems to happen. These are the times when we decide we are just going to give up, pack it in and go home. But it's at this time that Jesus tells us to *cast our nets yet one more time and see what happens.*

Just when you're ready to give up, Jesus says *try again.* Have you ever been to that point in your personal life and with your personal relationship to God and God's Word? Uncertain of where to go from here? Feeling that everything you do is either unappreciated, unimportant or wrong? Jesus says *keep trying...keep being yourself.* Jesus didn't tell the fishermen to go build a house. He told them to do what they knew best...continue to fish...and their nets were filled.

I think sometimes we lose sight of this fact. We assume that because everything isn't perfect that we are not doing the right thing. But God says, "*Just continue to work at being who you are. Continue to cast those nets and you will see a great return.*"

Then look at what happens after the fishermen cast their nets? The realization is so great that indeed they are in the presence of Jesus Christ the Messiah that they leave all that they have just received to follow Him.

This raises an interesting predicament for us today. If we give of ourselves to ministry through prayer and service and even financially and see that these are not working to help further the kingdom of God...we must do what we can and try even harder. Cast our nets yet one more time! And when the day comes that those nets return filled...we must be prepared to leave everything and follow our God.

In our modern day world, the way we can do this is to support with an even greater desire those very same ministries once again with our prayers, our time and our dollars.

Do you hear how serving our Lord works? If things are going bad, try *praying more, serving more and giving more.* And then when things go well we will want to *pray more, serve more, and give more!*

The time is here for each of us to cast our nets upon the waters of this life. *Amen.*

15

GROWING FAITH

SUGGESTED READING: MARK 7:24-30

I had just entered seminary and I had been hired as the youth worker at my new church a few weeks prior when I was asked to preach an afternoon service at the retirement home associated with the congregation. Of course I was nervous, because I had only preached two sermons in my life. Yet I realized this would be a great opportunity to practice my craft and deep down I believed the experience would do me good.

The text for that day's message was this passage from the Gospel of Mark. An unusual and perhaps even uncomfortable scripture lesson to be sure, and one I would not have chosen for myself if given a choice. Nevertheless this was the passage for the day and I was expected to use it. I delivered what I now consider a relatively basic message based upon my overly simplistic study at the time. We sang the final hymn, I gave the benediction and everybody began to disperse.

Then it happened. She rose to her feet, assisted by two nurses who were obviously there to tend to her every need. She made her way towards me in the back of the chapel. I had noticed her earlier in the service, in fact I recognized her from an earlier visit with the senior pastor of the church. Her presence was intimidating, yet I was glad she had made it a point to be there to hear me.

She was well into her 80's, a one-time school principal, a woman of education and authority...respected, and dare I say, even feared by her students and teachers for decades. Her credentials were beyond reproach. She was the type of person you noticed. It mattered not how many others were in the room when she was there, she was in charge. I am certain that over the years she became quite comfortable being the center of attention.

During our previous visit I noted that she was the only member the senior pastor did not address by her first name, until she informed him it was acceptable to do so. I remember also how in the midst of our visit, she grew thirsty and instructed the pastor to get her some water, which he promptly did. And when the time came and she tired, she simply told us it was time for us to go, and we rose and left.

Yes this woman was strong, educated and powerful. And she had made it a point to come and hear me preach! I wondered as she slowly made her way to the back of the chapel, did she enjoy the service, was she impressed with my illustrations, did she care for my speaking voice?

She approached me and said only one thing.

"Do you really think Jesus said that? I don't!"

I fumbled to find the proper response..."Well I suppose He did...after all it's in the Bible."

"Well I don't think He said it! Jesus wouldn't say anything so harsh and no one is going to convince me otherwise!" She wished me a good day and continued on her way.

The experience is as clear to me today as it was 30 years ago when it first occurred. I suppose it is a natural reaction, when faced with a rather uncomfortable and uncharacteristic statement on the part of Jesus. But I remember the words of St. Augustine, who once said, "If you believe what you like in the gospel and reject what you don't like; it is not the gospel you believe, but yourself."

We create a dangerous precedent if we only choose to listen to the words of Scripture we find comforting or agreeable. Often the words we most need to hear are those we are least comfortable hearing. It is therefore up to us not to deny the Words of Jesus, but to try to understand them.

Think about it, a seemingly desperate woman comes to Jesus for help in healing her daughter. If we take the time to understand the context of this encounter, Jesus' Words, which on the surface appear mean-spirited and rude to someone seeking help, can clearly be understood in a very different light.

The story follows the account of Jesus and His disciples being harassed by the Pharisees for not following the appropriate traditions. This passage follows the miracle of the feeding of the five thousand and Jesus walking on the water. In other words, much has taken place in a relatively short period of time in Jesus's ministry. Some have hypothesized that perhaps Jesus, at this point in His life, is stepping away from things in order to perhaps catch His breath as well as prepare for the work ahead.

If this were the case, it might make sense for Jesus to be a bit edgy, cranky and tired and respond harshly to any request of Him. No wonder He called the woman and her daughter *dogs*, a term of derision to the people of His day.

Dogs were considered to be unclean animals of the streets. *Jesus was just having a bad day,* some might say, *so give Him a break.*

But to think in such terms limits Jesus. Is it really possible for Jesus the Christ, Jesus the Son of God to act without compassion when dealing with anyone who genuinely seeks His aid? There surely must be a better answer.

It has often been noted that this is the only occasion in Jesus's ministry, that Jesus left Jewish territory. Sidon and Tyre were Gentile land. And while it is possible that Jesus left Jewish territory to find peace and quiet away from the Pharisees, another possibility is that His leaving Jewish land for the Gentile world was in fact a foreshadowing of the future. Remember the command of Jesus that the gospel must go out to the whole world? God's love was meant for all people. The Words of Jesus were not just for the Jew but for the Gentile also.

Yet even here Jesus was not free from the demands of human need. The Gospel of Matthew also includes this same story and there is value in noting it at this time.

Matthew 15:22 tells us, "A Canaanite woman from that region came out and started shouting, *'Have mercy on me, Lord, Son of David; my daughter is tormented by a demon.'* But He did not answer her at all, and His disciples came and urged Him saying *'send her away for she keeps shouting after us.'*"

A woman comes crying to Jesus and at first He appears to ignore her. But note that it is not Jesus, but rather the disciples who became annoyed and tell Jesus to give her what she wants just so they may get rid of her. While Mark fails to include this part of the story, it nevertheless makes sense. After all, Jesus is not encountering this woman alone, privately. She has entered a situation where others are watching every move and Word of Jesus.

Though it would seem that Jesus's reply is cold, we cannot doubt for a moment that Jesus has compassion for this woman. She is a Gentile and everyone there knows it. How can Jesus not only respond to this woman's request but also use the moment to make clear to all gathered that He has come for all God's children?

There was only one thing for Him to do. He had to use the situation. The woman was a Gentile but she was also a Greek. The Greeks were a people who had the *gift of conversation* - a love for banter, repartee, debate and mental sparring.

Jesus turned to her and said, *"It is not right to take the children's bread and throw it to the dogs."* Here is where a knowledge of the Greek is helpful, for if Jesus had said *dogs of the street*, it most certainly would have been an insult. Instead He uses the term better translated *puppies*. Anybody being cruel and critical would have used the other term. But Jesus is playing with the language, even as He is using the situation as a teaching moment. Jesus took the sting out of the word and in so doing the Greek woman knew immediately that she was with a friend.

The next point is critical. The woman's reply to Jesus was immediate, *"But even the dogs get their share of the crumbs which fall from their master's table."* How could Jesus not grant her the blessing and the healing she desired for her daughter? She came to Jesus, not out of desperation, but rather with *anticipation*. She came with a faith that He would enter into a relationship with her and she was prepared to respond to the Lord's challenge for her. She had a great faith. A faith that prepared her and a faith that would not be overcome.

This woman had faith, and because of this her daughter was healed. Isn't that wonderful? Healed because of her faith!

What does it mean for us today to have faith? And really, *what is faith?* When I have posed this question to others, many have difficulty verbalizing a response. Typically individuals conclude that faith is something we all have or should have as Christians, but as for what it is and why we should have it, the answers are not always so clear cut.

Nevertheless, it is absolutely essential that we understand precisely what it means to have faith and how to put faith to work in our lives as we make our individual journey to the cross. Otherwise, we are forced to live lives of desperation. Looking for quick fixes to life's challenges and Band-Aid approaches to life's pains.

The Syrophoenician woman offers us an extremely helpful example to follow. In her brief appearance in the gospel story we can see that faith is *something that grows.* Remember how this encounter with Christ unfolds. She comes to a man for help (in Matthew's gospel account she even refers to Jesus as, *Son of David*, a term of respect, but definitely an earthly title).

However, as she looks upon Jesus and enters into His life she sees something that cannot be expressed in earthly terms. She sees something divine and this is exactly what Jesus wanted to enlighten in this woman before He grants her request. "Someone once wrote of this story and described it as, *a request to a great man that was turned into a prayer to the living God.* And in the end she, and she alone, of all the persons in the Gospel of Mark, calls Jesus — *Lord!* Through this entire story we see this woman's faith clearly growing.

Now ask yourself, *is my faith growing? Why or why not?* The woman's faith, though obviously great to begin with...demonstrated by the simple fact that she confidently goes to Jesus in the first place; grows still more as her understanding of just who Jesus really is, is made known to her.

Where do you turn? Where do you go to find relationship with and grow in relationship to the living God? Again the example of this woman is so very helpful, for in her example we find a reminder that it is in *worship* that we can, should, and *must* grow in our relationship with Christ.

Consider that this woman began by following with her feet, and ended on her knees. She began with a request, and ended with a prayer. Whenever we come to Jesus, we must first come with praise of His majesty and only then with the statement of our own need.

How do you come to God in worship? *Do you worship in faith?* Celebrating God for who and what God is and ready to rejoice in God's presence? Do you come to the altar to encounter the risen Christ? Do you come to God in worship expecting to find God and have God challenge you in return?

A criticism that is often made of worship services is, *"I went and didn't get anything out of it."* Let us never make such statements if we cannot also be ready to answer, *"What did I put into it?"*

If we come to worship God with little or no expectation that God will respond, we shouldn't be surprised when nothing happens! We must come to God *expecting* a response. The woman was ready...when Jesus challenged her, there was not a moment's hesitation...no stuttering, no stammering...she was prepared...she knew that if she was to enter a relationship with Jesus she had best be prepared to respond.

How prepared are we when we come to God, that God might just seek us out to engage us?

Ultimately, faith must be persistent. This woman's faith was persistent and undeniable. So many people pray because they do not wish to miss the chance. They don't really believe in prayer. Instead, they have the feeling that by praying something *might just happen.* This is not the attitude to take. The woman in the story did not come to Jesus just because He was a possible help. *He was her only hope!* She came with *passionate hope* and a *refusal to be discouraged.* Prayer was not a ritual, it was the outpouring of the desire of a soul which felt that it could not, *must not,* take no for an answer.

Each of us must decide what we will do with our faith as we make our walk to the cross. It is clear that as Christians we all have faith, to one degree or another. We must remind ourselves, however, not be become comfortable with our faith. Jonathan Sherman once wrote, *"The enemy of faith is not doubt, but complacency."*

It is easy for human beings to sit back and become complacent about life. We tell ourselves that no matter what we do or how hard we try, things will come out the same in the end, be they good or bad. If the woman in the scripture had believed this, her daughter would not have been healed. Jesus said it, *for saying what you have said, for doing what you have done, the demon has left your daughter.*

We can't we sit back and expect our faith to grow on its own. We must step forward with confidence that a God of love seeks to enter our lives anew. We must come to God, not desperately grasping for help, but confidently reaching for the One who gives us hope. As we genuinely seek the Lord, our faith will not only grow, it will enable God to do great things *in us* and *through us*.

Today *(Originally written by Beah Richards)*

Today is ours, let's live it
And love is strong, let's give it
A song can help, let's sing it
And peace is dear, let's bring it
The past is gone, don't rue it
Our work is here, let's do it
Our world is wrong, let's right it
The battle hard, let's fight it
The road is rough, let's clear it
The future vast, don't fear it
Is faith asleep? Let's wake it
Today is ours, let's take it

16

EUTYCHUS

SUGGESTED READING: ACTS 20:7-12

I t was the spring semester at the seminary; the time of year when the weather begins to improve dramatically. It was also the time when the end of the school year was in sight and summer break would soon be arriving. The last thing anyone wanted to do was spend time in dark dreary classrooms. Because of this, it was a common practice for students to try to schedule classes that only met once per week during this semester. In order for the classes to meet only once per week, they lasted at least three hours at a time. But normally it was considered to be worth it in order to free up the rest of the week.

During my second year at school; the only such class available for me to take was an Ethics Course that began at 7 o'clock in the evening, taught by a professor who had been at the school so long it was rumored he knew several of the disciples personally.

In my opinion Christian Ethics courses are dull enough without the additional factor of a rather non dynamic professor. Anyone who has ever had to sit through long periods of uninteresting lecture, especially on warm spring evenings, understands what a challenge it can sometimes be; not only to keep your attention directed to what is going on, but merely to be able to stay awake at all.

Fortunately, this class met in one of the corner rooms on the second floor of the Administration Building at the seminary. The room had several large windows on two sides instead of just one. If you arrived early enough for class and took a seat in the corner of the room, you were at least assured a bit of a *cross breeze* that might help to keep you alert for the evening. An additional reason for sitting here was that if the class became too uninteresting, you could always look out onto the streets of East Liberty and find something going on to keep your attention.

Most of the term this worked perfectly for me; until one evening when the room was particularly warm, and the professor particularly dull--and--*I nodded off!* For how long, it is difficult to say. Now falling asleep in class is embarrassing enough, but while dozing I had one of those experiences we all have had at one time or another; when you dream that you're falling, and right before you hit the ground you wake up, usually with a jerk. Well that is what happened to me, and as I woke up, I slammed my hand down on the desktop in front of me. I immediately realized what had happened and began to clear my throat as if to say that I was listening all along and was just trying to make a point. My heart was racing. I was embarrassed. The only thing that made me feel better was that after I had calmed down and began to look around the room, I counted at least a half-dozen other students who were also asleep; dead to the world.

Since that time Eutychus, from Acts 20, and his exploits have been one of my favorites. Really for no other reason than the images that come to mind when the story is read.

It must be a true account of an actual event. Why else would Luke have gone to the trouble to share it. The described event has little or no bearing upon the rest of the story at this point; really there is no indication of why Eutychus sits where he sits, nor even that he is really dead when he hits the ground.

Bible scholars have used this passage from Acts to make several points, perhaps all valid. Some have even suggested that it is to warn the preacher about being long winded. If even the great preacher Paul can put the congregation to sleep by talking too long, just think what the modern day clergy are capable of.

Others have tried (without much convincing I might add) to say that this story points out that the crowd was so great that wanted to hear Paul, and Eutychus wished so desperately to be there that he was willing to do whatever was necessary to be in that room. And that it was only after being overcome by the heat of the room that he fell from the third story to the ground.

No, in my opinion Eutychus is an example of something we are all guilty of at times, the same thing that I was guilty of in that ethics class; a lack of real interest in what was going on. I think the only reason Eutychus finds himself sitting in that window is because he's thinking to himself, well if this guy is boring, at least I can watch what is going on out in the street, or maybe the fresh air will keep me awake.

How often have you wished there were clear glass windows in a sanctuary so as to be able to do something else when the sermon gets a little long and a little boring? I wonder if there was perhaps some secret conspiracy centuries ago by a bunch of dull uninteresting clergy to use stained glass windows in their churches to keep the congregations from drifting. Some have used this story to say that Paul has performed a great miracle in raising the dead. But really the story never says this. It says that the people think he is dead, but that Paul when he looks at him tells them that he is alive.

Perhaps this is my more cynical side showing through but I can't help but wonder if perhaps the reason Eutychus is lying there acting dead is because he's so embarrassed that he fell asleep in the first place.

The real point of the story, in my opinion, has to do with one issue...*listening*; or better yet, *paying attention*. The reason Eutychus fell asleep and fell out of the window was that his attention was not fully upon what Paul was saying. In fact I wouldn't be surprised if he wasn't listening at all.

There is a story told that Franklin Roosevelt got tired of smiling and repeating the usual things at White House receptions. So, one evening he decided to find out whether anybody was paying attention to what he was saying. As each person came up to him with extended hand, he flashed a big smile and said, "I murdered my grandmother this morning." People would automatically respond with comments such as "How lovely" or "Just continue the great work." Nobody listened to what he was saying except one foreign diplomat. When the president said, "I murdered my grandmother this morning," the diplomat responded softly, "I'm sure she had it coming to her."

The fact is that very few people listen anymore...*really listen*...and fewer yet ever bring the listening skills they have to their relationship with God.

There are at least three areas where we as Christians have the opportunity to come to and be in a relationship with God; through other Christians, through church, and through prayer. Yet in any of these relationships, just how good are we at *really listening?*

When it comes to relating to one another, how often do we really try to listen to what others are saying. When you greet someone and ask, "How are you today?" do you *really* want to know, and do you *really listen* for their reply?

Ask yourself, when someone is your friend, are they your friend because you take the time to listen to their concerns, or is it because they take the time to listen to you?

Not long ago I had the privilege of assisting with the funeral service of a very dear friend, Bill. Bill was one of those people that we all know, that loved to talk. In fact I have never met another person that could remember the details of a story, or who could paint so clear a word picture than could Bill.

He could start off talking about World War II, shift to a few stories about his grandfather the painter, and without a moment's hesitation conclude with another twenty minutes about the light company from which he had retired.

Because of Bill I know more about WWII and light companies than I probably ever wanted to know. Yet it wasn't until after Bill's death that I realized something very special about the way he remembered and would tell a story. Bill's stories and remembrances were always filled with very specific, even minute details about the individuals that he came into contact with. He could tell you, not only the name of the person in his story, but the person's age as well, what he was wearing, where he lived, his wife's maiden name, what they did later in life, where he lived now, and so on and so forth. As I said, we all know people that like to tell stories, but the detail with which Bill told them says something to me. In order to be able to remember all those details, he had to take the time to find them out in the first place. More importantly, he had to care enough about the people involved to remember them.

You know it's funny, because most of the time those individuals who are great talkers are very seldom good listeners. Yet it's obvious that was not the case with Bill. In order to remember the way he did, he must have been doing an awful lot of listening, maybe even while he was talking!

Are we able to listen to others, or do we do all the talking in our relationships?

There is a poem that I believe puts it quite nicely. It says:

His thoughts were slow, his words were few,
and never formed to glisten.
But he was a joy to all his friends,
you should have heard him listen!

The next place we can find a fuller relationship with God through listening, is in our prayer life. There was a five year old girl attending a wedding and sitting with her grandmother. She had never been in a church service before. During the wedding, the minister said: "Let us pray." Each person bowed his or her head in prayer. The little girl looked around and saw all the heads bowed and eyes turned toward the floor and she cried: "Grandmother, what are they all looking for?" Indeed, what are we looking for when we pray? If we are looking for guidance through this life, if we are looking for answers to concerns of our hearts, why do we spend *so much time talking at God* and *so little time quietly listening for God's reply?*

Silently now I wait for Thee, ready my God, Thy will to see, open my ears illumine me, Spirit Divine! God is speaking, are we listening?

The third place we can listen for God is in church. But I think perhaps, surprisingly, this is the most difficult place of all. Mostly because, we don't like to come to church to hear where we fall short, so much as we like to be assured that we are doing what is right. I've actually heard people say that they don't want to hear social issues raised in the pulpit. They reason, *I work out in the real world during the week and I don't need someone telling me what I should be doing about issues like hunger, abuse, abortion and gay rights.* But if we aren't to raise those issues in church, where will we? Then there are issues within the church like stewardship, tithing, and missions that we don't want to bring up because we are afraid of hurting other's feelings. Perhaps the reason we don't like to hear or raise certain topics in church is that we are afraid of what the response might be.

We are like the rather non-religious hunter who was out one Sunday morning hunting bears. As he trudged through the forest looking for bears, he came upon a large steep hill. He climbed the hill and just as he was pulling himself up over the last of the outcropping of rocks, a huge bear met him nose to nose. The bear roared fiercely. The man was so scared that he lost his balance and fell down the hill with the bear not far behind. On the trip down the hill the man lost his gun. When he finally stopped tumbling, he found that he had a broken leg. Escape was impossible and so the man, prayed: "God if you will make this bear a Christian I will be happy with whatever lot you give me for the rest of my life." The bear was no more than three feet away from the man when it stopped dead in its tracks, looked up to the heavens quizzically, and then fell to its knees and prayed in a loud voice; "Lord bless this food of which I am about to partake. Amen."

The man's prayer was answered but not exactly the way he intended it to be.

Aren't we like that in the church?

Preach fire and brimstone preacher! Tell it the way it is! Make sure *they all know* what *they are doing wrong.* We never want to hear where it is that perhaps *we* fall short.

Listening. The need to listen for God in every aspect of our lives, and to not allow ourselves to become distracted with what is going on outside the window. To listen for God working in our life is absolutely essential, or else we too, like Eutychus, will fall, only our fall will be greater than three stories.

If and when the day comes that we as Christians individually, and we as the church collectively, truly challenge ourselves to listen to our God, God's world, and God's children, then and only then will be able to begin to change it. As the people of God let us vow to listen for what God has in store for us. *Amen.*

PART III DISCUSSION QUESTIONS

1. Why is it so hard to *let go* of the baggage of life?
2. Would you be more content in life if you truly believed that *you* didn't have to have all the answers?
3. When you are feeling discouraged, what helps to lift your spirit?
4. How difficult is it for you to take Jesus at His Word?
5. Where do you most often *listen* for God?

PART IV

LESSONS ALONG
THE WAY

Over the course of our lives God entrusts others to our care: children, aging parents, friends and coworkers. Certainly, when this occurs it is our responsibility to nurture, support, encourage and sometimes even care for them. But the interesting thing is that if we are open and paying attention, we might just learn a thing or two from them in return.

17

FRONT PORCHES AND BACKYARDS

SUGGESTED READING: ACTS 16:16-34

A re you a front porch person or a backyard person? Little difference you say? Nothing could be further from the truth. Certainly there are some similarities between the two. Each involves enjoying the outdoors, and yes, it is possible to entertain in either place; but beyond this there is much to be said regarding the differences.

Front porch people, are those persons who sit out front and take in all that goes by. Front porch people watch the cars and bicyclists speed past the house, they watch the dog walkers and joggers lap the block, they nod and wave to passersby and even issue an invitation with a hand gesture for others to come and chat with friends or family. Front porch people seem to anticipate and look forward to seeing new things and new people. They watch for them. It is easy to approach front porch people. Many almost expect it. Front porch people have a way of making you feel at home.

When our children were little our family would spend one week each summer at Chautauqua, New York. Chautauqua, is a community of homes built in the earlier part of the last century, many with two or three stories of front porches. The first time we vacationed there on our first day we decided to take the children for a walk through the community to see the sights. Our son Aaron was three at the time, and Aaron was never bashful. As we walked those porch-lined streets of Chautauqua, we came upon, time and again *front porch people* who would wave and smile. Aaron would inevitably wave and respond, "*Hello! This is my mommy and this is my daddy and we are happy to be here!*"

After a few blocks of this you would have thought Aaron were running for Mayor of Chautauqua (he might have won too!) But he was simply responding to the attitude that is so often exhibited by *front porch people*.

Backyarders are a slightly different breed, and I confess that I am typically much more the backyarder in my personal life. Backyarders, view their backyards as places to go to *be alone* to *get away to*. We build fences or plant hedges that separate us from, or at least keep at a safe distance, our neighbors. We keep our children from the busyness of the front yard and street because it is not safe with all those fast cars and big dogs. We hide away in the pretend quiet of the backyard, with our gas grills, our shaded picnic tables, swing sets and vegetable gardens.

Subsequently, backyards are not nearly as inviting to others as are front porches. You must be invited into someone's backyard. As in "*Why don't you and your wife come over sometime?*" You earn that invitation. And if someone enters your backyard without your invitation, you feel uncomfortable, and perhaps even unsafe.

Finally, while front porch sitters seem to anticipate new things. Backyarders sometimes seem to seek out the creation of a world that will not change. You never hear someone say, "Not on my front porch!" It is not by coincidence that the phrase is "Not in *my* backyard!" It is so very often uttered by persons who do not want change in their community, or world, if it is going to directly disturb their own immediate existence.

Yes, it is great that our community can offer a drug rehabilitation center...just don't put it in *my* backyard. Oh it's wonderful that we are able to house the homeless... just don't build your shelter close enough to my house that it will negatively impact *my* property values. Such attitudes are the feelings of backyarders in this life. Do your thing, as long as it doesn't impact *me.*

Let me share with you a personal experience from my childhood. The year was 1972. Like many children who grew up in and around the Pittsburgh region, one of my favorite weekend morning shows to watch was Paul Shannon's Castle.

Each telecast had Paul and a set of bleachers filled with Cub Scouts, Girl Scouts and grade school classes from the greater Pittsburgh area. They would applaud and cheer as Three Stooges shorts and Kimba the White Lion cartoons were shown to the viewers at home.

Every summer Paul Shannon would encourage children to raise money for muscular dystrophy by hosting backyard carnivals. Oftentimes those same kids would then get to appear on the broadcast. With this in mind, the kids in our neighborhood in Duncansville; Bill, Eric, Mike, Sean, Chris, Jim, Tom, Rick, Dave, and others, discussed the idea of holding our very own carnival.

We talked with our parents and one after another they said, "Oh that is a great idea, go for it!" Then we would ask one parent after another, "Can we have it in your yard?"

and one after another came the responses, "*Not in my backyard!* You're not messing up my yard for something like that!"

That is until I asked my parents. We had the smallest yard of any of my friends so we didn't think it was the best place to hold a carnival, but when I asked, they said "Yes!"

A few weeks later, that yard was filled with games and contests, clowns, and magic acts, rides and food, everyone had a great time, and that small group of third and fourth graders were able to raise over one hundred dollars that first year, and even more the following year when we did it again. And it all happened in our backyard!

The scripture from Acts has a perfect example of Paul dealing with the backyarders of Philippi. Paul and Silas are in the community for some time, praying and publicly preaching about Jesus Christ, and no one seems to mind one bit. But then something interesting happens. A woman possessed by a demon keeps following Paul and Silas yelling at the top of her lungs, "These men are servants of the Most High God, who proclaim to you the way of salvation." After some days, Paul says to the spirit "I order you in the Name of Jesus Christ to *come out of her.*" And it does.

There is just one problem with this; since the spirit no longer possesses her, she is no longer able to read palms, tell fortunes and provide entertainment for all the business conventions being held in Philippi. Once her owners become aware of this they are furious!

The owners of this slave girl, who just happen to be the chief officers of the "Greater Philippi Homeowners Association", a group of people who could have cared less what Paul and Silas were doing until that day, immediately take them to court. "These men are disturbing our city and are advocating customs that are not lawful for us as Romans to adopt or observe." If this were really their concern, they would have voiced it much earlier. No, their concern was that Paul and Silas were disturbing their backyard existence, changing the world they had come to expect, and they wanted none of it.

Let us be clear about a very significant point. It is not Paul or Silas who disturb these backyard dwellers of Philippi. No, it is *Jesus Christ*. It is not Paul that causes the demon to leave the girl, it is Jesus.

Our Lord has a way of doing that, you know. Entering into the contented lives we have created for ourselves and turning things upside down.

Oftentimes, dear friends, Jesus doesn't wait for an invitation to do so. Saul was quite content persecuting Christians and bringing them bound in chains to Jerusalem. For Saul it couldn't get any better than that. His world was complete. Then Jesus encountered him on the road to Damascus and changed his world.

I guess the real problem with backyards is that so often they just aren't *real*.

Now don't get me wrong. The backyard certainly *is* comfortable. In fact it is quite relaxing and enjoyable to sit there and take in what surrounds me. But if I were to stay in my own backyard the whole summer long, I might begin to think that all there is in the world are happy children, green grass and shade giving trees. Families that enjoy playing, cooking and sharing together. That is all I can see from my own vantage point upon the world I have created for myself in my own backyard.

As much as I would like that to be the case, I realize that once I go out my front door into the real world, I know that life is not so beautiful everywhere. Pollution ravages some parts of the world. The rain forests are disappearing at an alarming rate, civil unrest continues in other parts of the world, and children are killing children in our own country on what seems to be an almost weekly basis.

Backyarders wish to protect a way of life and maintain a status quo even if the reality is not as rosy as they would like to convince themselves that it is. After yet another recent shooting that made the national news, a poster was displayed in that community, "If it can happen here it can happen anywhere."

If we sit back as a community and pretend that acts of violence and evil are not possible in the backyard existence we have created, we are sadly mistaken. The reality of this life is that sin and evil can be found everywhere. Paul and Silas found it in a young woman on the way to church. We see it, if we open our eyes in the paper, on the news, at work, in school, and in our own lives.

The truth is that even the "idealized" worlds that some create for themselves are not nearly as perfect as we would like to believe. Take for instance my own backyard. I previously noted that I can sit in comfort and see my green grass, gas grill, swing set and children at play. But the reality is, that there are many weeds growing in that yard that need to be pulled, the grill needs to be cleaned, the swing set is in constant need of repair, and the children I protect from the front yard and street, fall and get cut and bruised in the backyard as well. You see, things are never as perfect as we would like them to be.

Now ask yourself, do you lead a front porch or a backyard existence? Do you wake up each day, looking forward to the new and different; perhaps even challenging aspects of life that might come your way. Are you willing and able to reach out to those in need before they ask for it? Are you unwilling to accept that everything must always be the way it has always been? Are you willing to believe that it isn't necessary to settle for mediocrity in this life, but instead strive for perfection? Then you are poised on the front porch of life.

Or do you wish to stay in the backyard, comfortable, satisfied, with blinders on to the needs of others and your own ability to make a difference for yourself and the world? Attitudes such as this ultimately enslave us, and those backyards of comfort can easily become cells of entrapment.

There is good news today, dear friends, for the One Who loosed the chains and opened the doors for Paul and Silas, the One Who opened the eyes of Saul, the One Who cast out a demon from a young girl, can enter into our lives anew at any moment and free us as well.

I remind you that often when Christ enters into our lives, He chooses the backyards of our existence, the places where we are most comfortable and contented. It seems as if our earth quakes, but how else can prisoners be set free?

Let us be thankful that Christ is not only in my backyard and yours, but He is also on the front porch, in our homes, and in our hearts. Loving us and challenging us to serve and follow faithfully in all that we do. *Amen.*

18

CONSIDER THE LILIES

SUGGESTED READING: MATTHEW 6:24-34

I remember the grave marker quite clearly; it was an approximately 4 feet tall, white obelisk shape. It was well worn from years of harsh weather, and it leaned ever so slightly. We visited it in preparation for Memorial Day each year...we, meaning me, my grandmother, mother, and my brother. Like many families, we took flowers to the markers of deceased family members; except for this one. We never planted flowers there, not once in all the years I remember going. Oh, it wasn't that we didn't care, it was actually quite the opposite.

This tombstone, marked the final resting place of John Kantner, my grandmother's grandfather. He had fought in the Civil War. My grandmother told me once he never spoke much about his experience, only that he did what he needed to do.

He had died in the late 1890's and the family had a marker set in the ground. By the time I was making yearly visits to the cemetery with family it was the 1960's. I can remember the American flag that waved in front of the old stone marker. I remember how weathered the letters were on the soft stone used... But what I remember the most were the flowers. See we didn't plant flowers because there were already flowers there. Each and every year, a large group of Tiger Lilies bloomed all around this grave marker. Of course the orange flowers would not appear until later in the summer, but each spring we would take notice of the flowers starting to spring forth.

No one in the family remembered when they were planted or who had planted them, but each year they bloomed. I don't know much about gardening and flowers and I don't know if this is common or not, I just remember that for me this was one of the signs that summer was coming. Then one day each summer we would return to the cemetery and view the numerous beautiful orange tiger lilies blooming around the grave of my great grandfather. A man, my grandmother told me, who always did what he was supposed to do.

Isn't it strange that despite the tremendous achievements of modern civilization we are more worried about our lives than ever before? Take the advances in the medical sciences for instance: problems with heart disease, infectious diseases, and even cancer can be treated more successfully today than ever before. Or think about all the security devices: fire-alarms, insurance against all sorts of catastrophes and eventualities, inspections to make transportation safe, air and water clean, hospitals antiseptic, restaurant food healthy and, my personal favorite: checking account overdraft-protection. All of these things are designed to allow us to breathe easier and be less worried about life.

Yet, the early 21st century has been dubbed the "age of anxiety" because people in the Western hemisphere, including you and I, tend to worry about our lives and future more than ever before.

More than 20 years ago Bobby McFerrin's song entitled "Don't worry, be happy!" became such a hit. Remember the song? I assume it must have been the words because it certainly couldn't have been the music that made it successful. People realize that they need some remedy, some way to deal with their worries. But does this message really bring a remedy? "Don't worry--be happy." That sounds easy, but how exactly do we do that?

When was the last time you worried about something? In all likelihood it probably hasn't been very long since you last felt anxious or concerned about something in your life. Let me ask, when you were anxious, when you were worried, was your first thought to tell God "Thank You"?

The Apostle Paul speaks frequently, in so many words, of the benefit that comes from demonstrating an attitude of gratitude.

"First of all, then, I urge that supplications, prayers, intercessions, and thanksgiving be made for everyone, for kings and all who are in high positions, so that we may lead a quiet and peaceable life in all godliness and dignity." 1 Timothy 2:1

In the Old Testament we find the words of the Psalmist speaking to this attitude as well. *"The LORD has done great things for us, and we rejoiced." Psalm 126:3*

And then of course we read of Jesus looking at a couple of birds and reminding those with ears to hear, *don't worry, if God takes care of them, won't He also care for you?*

It almost seems that an attitude of gratitude is the antithesis to fear and worries. As we are freed from worries, as our gratitude to God overflows, we will find ourselves able to reach out to others; to people that may be worry-stricken, to the poor, the needy, those of us who are oppressed, suffering under the wages of sin and need to be defended.

I haven't lived in central Pennsylvania for 35 years, but let me tell you what happened the last time I visited the Carson Valley Cemetery outside of Duncansville, Pennsylvania.

It was approximately 20 years ago, I pulled into the parking area next to the cemetery with my kids to show them the family markers. I was positive I could remember where the stone was, but we couldn't find it. Around and around we walked. It was a four foot high obelisk! Surely it should stand out! Up and down the rows of the corner section of the cemetery we walked until I realized what had happened.

From a distance of a few hundred yards, I could see the old marker...*it had fallen over!* The large pointed stone that had once proudly marked the grave of a veteran had toppled over. I was saddened and disappointed. How long ago had it occurred? Why hadn't anyone done something about it? Maybe the cemetery didn't have any records to contact descendants... who knows?

As we made our way to the stone we were stopped in our tracks at the most incredible site. Still blooming on the opposite side of the marker was...you guessed it...a few small orange tiger lilies. I thought to myself, even if we forget, God remembers!

It occurs to me that there are many things in life we can choose to worry about. It is our choice. We can do our best to do what is right...live and love and care and share our faith. And when called upon, to serve and fight against sin. And trust that in all things God is watching over us.

 Consider the lilies of the field, how they grow; they neither toil nor spin, yet I tell you, even Solomon in all his glory was not arrayed like one of these. (Matt. 6:28-29)

19

TAKE THE PLUNGE

SUGGESTED READING: ROMANS 8:31-39

Do you consider yourself an optimist or a pessimist? Is your cup in life half-empty, or is it half-full? What is your attitude towards your life, and more importantly your life in Christ? There are numerous images that quickly come to mind, many of them relating to water. Is your life one of sinking or swimming, going with the flow, riding the waves, changing with the tide, feeling as though you are in over your head, or my focus for this chapter, taking the plunge! Plunge as in *plunge right in to something...and get to it!*

Have you ever wondered why it is that so many people in this life walk around with heads bowed low, with heavy hearts and seemingly without a reason to get up in the morning?

The reality is life is tough! It's hard and it's not always fair. The kindest and most loving people do not always have that love returned. The most generous and giving people in life do not always have the same returned to them either. Why is that? I don't know. What I do know is that there are no guarantees in life. Nevertheless we must do what we can to not only get through and but also to enjoy ourselves along the way.

I'm a great fan of the late actress Judy Garland. Garland's life was cut short by a drug overdose, following many years of hardship. Of course Judy is best known for one particular song. Who doesn't remember the sweet teenage Dorothy in the Wizard of Oz singing that song of hope regarding what the future could possibly hold in store for her, *Somewhere Over the Rainbow*?

Ironically, if you ever listen to a recording of that song, sung by this same talented vocalist late in her life; you can actually hear the sadness in her voice. Even as she sings the very same words as she did as a child, the tone of her voice is such that you get the impression that she no longer sings about the hope of getting to that place over the rainbow, but rather of a hopelessness and heart wrenching agony that even though happy little bluebirds fly beyond the rainbow...why can't I?

Judy Garland, like so many others, is one who ultimately was in over her head, overwhelmed by this life. I don't know exactly what it is that overwhelms some people and not others. All I know is that it is possible to learn from others mistakes and successes.

I also know that as a Christian, I can be assured-- *promised*--that neither death nor life, nor angels nor demons, present or future powers, heights, depths or anything else will be able to separate me from the love of God. With that assurance, life, even at its most challenging, can become bearable.

I love the Steve Martin movie of several decades ago, Parenthood. The movie was about the trials and tribulations of a multigenerational family all living in the same community together. At one critical point in the film when

Steve Martin is at his wits end concerning things at work, at home, and life in general; his very elderly grandmother makes the following observation:

"Some people like the merry-go-round; but I like the roller-coaster! The rollercoaster has excitement and energy. Yes it has its ups and downs but that's what makes it so thrilling! On the other hand the merry-go-round just goes in circles!"

Some would say that a life like a merry-go-round might be considered comfortable and safe; but perhaps a little uninteresting as well.

On the other hand a rollercoaster life has its ups and downs, thrills and chills, frightening moments, times of exhilaration. Someone who rides the rollercoaster of life and enjoys it, is someone who is willing to plunge right in and do it! Such people are adventurous to be sure.

I remember an adult Sunday school class having a discussion about risk takers, and challenges one Sunday. I was commenting that I had always considered myself rather adventurous, at which point my *always supportive wife* sighed loudly from across the room. *"Oh please Mark, I've known you for twenty years and the most adventurous thing you have ever done was to go to the MALL on a Saturday afternoon!*

My wife's comments notwithstanding, it is clear that some people feel you have to be willing and able to bungee jump from a bridge or skydive in order to be considered adventurous and one who is willing to take the plunge and dive right in so to speak.

Sometimes, however, taking the plunge, means fully immersing yourself in something that is perhaps not intense and exhilarating but is, nevertheless, significant. Taking care of a sick loved one, leaving work to raise a family, changing careers in mid-life from something you make money at, but don't really love, to a job that is enriching, fulfilling, challenging, and helpful to others.

And while the parent who stays home and takes care of the children, or the child who welcomes into his or her home an aging parent, to care for them, may not view themselves as adventurous. Such people surely have *the right stuff*, as they say, for it is in and through such acts that they have *taken the plunge.*

To plunge right in, could imply, not thinking about what you're doing...being impulsive, or unprepared, not paying attention. I remember a few years ago, my entire family went with the youth of our church on a summer work camp experience in North Carolina.

Outside the lodge where we stayed was a small shallow pond. One afternoon, after a hard day's work, some youth came running in, screaming that a little boy had just fallen into this pond. Without even looking up, Karen and I said at the exact same time, *"Oh, that's our son Aaron."* Sure enough a few seconds later Aaron stuck his soaking wet head around the corner waving to us. *Sorry!*

Aaron took the plunge, not because he was prepared to, but because he was unprepared and not paying attention.

The type of person we should each endeavor to be, however, is not someone who acts without thinking. Instead we should be willing to plunge right in, after counting the cost, and understanding the sacrifice that is needed.

What areas of your life have you plunged into in the past, in the sense that you gave your all to them, you counted the cost, knew the risk and went for it anyway? I assure you if you are able to lead your life in such a fashion, not foolhardy and haphazard, but committed and intentional, you will be a happy person. If so, even the trials, the dips in the rollercoaster of life, will still be tolerable.

In this moment, consider what type of attitude you bring to your relationship with Jesus. When it comes to Christ, have you or can you take the plunge and understand the costs and still be willing to enter into a deeper and more complete relationship with Him?

Far too often we jump into a relationship with Jesus without much thought. Without giving it serious consideration, but simply doing it because others have, or because we think we should, but without really understanding why we should desire that very same relationship with Him.

If you're not sure how you would categorize your relationship with Jesus, ask yourself this question:

Is my relationship with Christ something I view as safe or does it offer challenges and thrills along with frightening moments and even hardships?

The late great religious thinker and writer, Leslie Newbiggin, once wrote that believing in Jesus, or *being converted,* as he put it "does not mean merely the transfer from one self-centered religious community to another. Nor does it mean only finding one's own personal peace with God. It means being so changed that you become an agent of change."

We might state it this way. When we plunge into a true relationship with Jesus Christ, we can't stop ourselves from encouraging others to do the same.

Remember when your parents would say to you, "well if all your friends jumped off a bridge would you do it too?" Well for us, it should be, *if I truly take the plunge, I won't be satisfied until all my friends have done so also.*

Newbiggin also said, however, "When you ask what is the purpose of making converts, the answer is, so they can make more coverts, and when you ask what is the purpose of those further converts, it is so they can make more converts. There is, in other words, an infinite regress. And, as we know from the medical analogy, the multiplication of cells unrelated to the purpose of the body is what we call cancer. That's a very hard thing to say, and I don't want to suggest that the folks who are in the Church growth school are blind to these points. But I do think that a very sharp criticism needs to be made against the idea that the Church exists simply to make more members, irrespective of the purpose for which the Father sent the Son into the world, which is that the presence of the reign of God might be a reality now."

Religion is not, cannot, and must not, be simply about bringing large numbers of people to Church. Jesus is concerned about a single number...one. Each and every... one of *us*...and each and every one of *them* out in the world.

We must do all that we can, to plunge into a relationship with Christ, and in so doing, ready ourselves to share Him with the world. I have always loved the words attributed to the Missionary to Africa, Louise Robinson Chapman, which could be a rallying call for any and all who are willing to enter into such a relationship with God:

"I'm part of the fellowship of the unashamed. I have Holy Spirit power. The die has been cast. I have stepped over the line. The decision has been made. I'm a disciple of His. I won't look back, let up, slow down, back away or be still.

My past is redeemed, my present makes sense, my future is secure. I'm finished and done with low living, sight walking, small planning, smooth knees, colorless dreams, tame visions, mundane talking, cheap living, and dwarfed goals.

I no longer need preeminence, prosperity, position, promotions, plaudits, or popularity. I don't have to be right, first, tops, recognized, praised, regarded or rewarded. I now live by faith, lean on His presence, walk by patience, lift by prayer, and labor by power.

I won't give up, shut up, let up, until I have stayed up, stored up, prayed up, paid up, preached up for the cause of Christ. I am a disciple of Jesus. I must go till He comes, give till I drop, preach till all know and work till He stops me. And when He comes for His own, He will have no problem recognizing me—my banner will be clear.

I remember a day many years ago when our, still little, son Joshua was just a few years old and playing on a jungle gym. He was happy and laughing until he came to the slide. When he saw how high he was, he was unsure of what to do next. His childish excitement quickly turned to nervous fear as he began to cry "Daddy!" But once he was assured that we were there to help him, he slid away with reckless abandon. We can all do the same. *Nothing* in all creation can separate us from the love of God in Christ Jesus our Lord. For our Heavenly Parent is there to help us as we go forward. It's time to plunge on in, the water's fine. *Amen.*

20

BELONGING

LUKE 19:1-10

Twenty plus years ago I attended a minister's conference in Toronto. The meeting room in which we met for most of the seminars easily held over 800 people. The speakers for the entire week were tremendous and the worship was inspiring. I must admit, however, to one day becoming a bit frustrated and annoyed with one particular gentleman who happened to be sitting a few rows over and maybe a row ahead of me.

Now if we were to be honest we all have little things about others that annoy us at times. Whether it is the tone of someone's voice, a pompous attitude they display, or even the type of clothing they choose to wear. Even though we know we are not supposed to, we often judge a book by its cover.

Well, it just so happens that this particular man was engaged in one of those things that drives me up a wall. He was a gum chomper! Now don't get me wrong, I don't mind if someone chews gum normally, but this guy was not your normal everyday gum chewer. He was one of those people who chews gum as if his very life depends on it. His mouth moved up and down like a piston, his jaw went from right to left with regularity. Just about every fifteen minutes or so he would pull out his supply and shove yet another piece into his already overflowing mouth.

And yes, I understand that it shouldn't bother me. But we all have little idiosyncrasies that get on our nerves and this just happens to be one that irritates me. Probably the only two things that irritate me more are those people who sit behind you in movie theaters and crunch ice, or that student in every class or gathering that feels it is necessary to answer every rhetorical question the teacher asks.

You know what I mean, when the history teacher begins her lecture, "Have you ever considered what the world would be like if the Germans had won World War II?" Now everybody in the class knows they are supposed to think about this and consider it, but there is always *one guy* that feels the need to raise his hand and say, "Why no ma'am, I never did consider what that would be like..." These guys drive me nuts...but anyway...back to our gum chomper!

This fellow bugged me so much, rightly or wrongly, that I was bound and determined not to be anywhere near him the next morning; so much so, that I made a point of arriving a half hour before everybody else. I found a nice seat towards the front of the 800 seat hall, completely away from where he was sitting the day before, and as soon as I sat down, this same guy came chomping into the room and sat down three seats away from me!

Well, I thought about it and thought about it. This really isn't that big of a deal, I should just sit here and ignore him, but I know I can't and he is going to distract my attention from the lectures. So I got up and moved to the other side of the room and enjoyed the morning.

During our afternoon session that day, we broke up into smaller groups. The class I was meeting with was in a smaller conference room that held about 100 people. Again I arrived early to get a good seat. Some books were on the seat beside me. I gave them no mind. Very rapidly the room filled, all except the seat right beside me. Then, just before the speaker stood up to give his lecture, the doors flew open and one more person entered the room....you guessed it...the gum chomper and guess where he had put his books? Right next to me! *God works in mysterious ways to be sure.*

Well, I knew that I couldn't possibly move this time, so I decided I would simply *not look at him;* I would stare straight ahead and concentrate on the speaker. The only problem was that the walls of this room were covered with mirrors and from where I was sitting regardless, of whatever mirror I looked into, guess who I saw? *Him again!*

I was sure that he would annoy me the rest of the afternoon; then the speaker began his talk by saying, "Have you ever considered what your life would be like if you did not have Christ as your personal Savior," and, *I swear this is true*, the guy right in front of me raised his hand and said, "You know I have never really considered that...blah blah blah"...and as he was rambling away the woman sitting directly behind me, began to crunch away on her glass of ice chips that she had brought with her for the day.

All I could do at that point was smile and begin to laugh, as I thought...God does indeed have a sense of humor. For what He was obviously telling me was not to worry about such foolish things and to recognize the more important fact that we were all there together to grow in Christ. When we gather together as the children of God we need to do so recognizing that all the other distractions of this world are just that, *distractions,* and only if we allow them to be.

How sad it is that so often in life we allow ourselves to become distracted, and to lose focus on what is truly important. Finding and experiencing the love of God in our lives and then sharing it with others is what is important.

There is a passage of scripture which is regularly promoted at sporting events, John 3:16: *"For God so loved the world that He gave His only begotten Son, that whosoever believes in Him should not perish but have eternal life."*

Do we really give thought to what that means? After all, why does God love the world? Certainly, He created it; but look at all the rotten things we have done over time. He placed Adam and Eve in the garden of Eden, "All this is for you ...just one thing...don't eat from that tree". And what do they do? Eat from that tree!

Cain and Abel are brothers who are expected to watch out for each other. And Cain kills Abel. Lot and his family are being led away from the sinful cities of Sodom and Gomorrah and God explains "I will save you...just one thing...don't turn around and look back." And sure enough, Lot's wife cannot resist and turns around and turns into a pillar of salt. Later, the Israelites are led out of slavery in Egypt. God instructs them "Have no other Gods before me" and at the very same time, they are hard at work making a golden calf to worship.

The list could go on and on. God keeps giving humans chances, and we keep throwing them away! So why then does God love us?

Ask yourself this, do you love your children? As you're dragging a screaming child out of a grocery store, while every other shopper looks at you as though you are the worst parent in the world, or as your teenager slams his door behind him as he ignores what you are saying to him, or as the baby cries from 11 o'clock at night until 5 o'clock in the morning, in any of these cases do you find yourself saying *how much you love these children*? I doubt it! Yet you know that deep down *you do have love in your heart for them*, but if it isn't because of how they behave, or how they listen, there can only be one reason that you love them. It is because they are *yours*. You love your kids because they are *yours!* And God loves us because we are *His* children...it is that simple!

So let's review, God knows us. He knows everything about us. And still He loves us. How much does He love us? Enough to send His Son Jesus to die for us. And why does Jesus die for us? To take away our sin and offer us eternal life with Him in heaven.

I am reminded of the story about the minister who had a bad experience with the church he was serving. The people were unloving and mean spirited. Nothing ever went right, and finally he became so disgusted with the un-Christian attitudes of its members that he began to look for another position. After some time, he found a job as the head chaplain at the state penitentiary. For his final sermon with that congregation he used John 14:2, "I go to prepare a place for you so that where I am you may be also!"

We need to remember that when Christ uttered these same words, what He was telling those who believed in Him, was that He was going to heaven to prepare a place for them there.

So Jesus comes, lives, dies and rises from the dead and because of that we too have the promise of eternal life. That's great news, is it not? Because of what Christ has done for us...we belong to Him.

Belonging: being recognized as belonging to someone or something, is very important to us all. From an early age we all want to and try very hard to *belong*. Maybe it's because we are in need of feeling that we are *needed and wanted*. Consider all the groups that we join during our lives. When young we join the Cub Scouts, Brownies, Boy Scouts, Girl Scouts, Camp Fire Girls, and sports teams. When we are a little older we join fraternities and sororities.

When older yet; lodges, the Masons, the Elks, the Moose, the Shriners, the Eastern Star, women's' clubs, Lions, Rotary, Kiwanis, the list can go on and on. And while we can make the claim that each organization provides a service, either to its members or to the community, there is one thing that is common to all of these groups. None could exist without its *members*. All groups and organizations must operate under the premise that individuals will want to be members of the group.

The story of Zacchaeus is an example of just such a situation. Being chief of the tax collectors would make him a very unpopular man in any age, but particularly in this time because such men were almost always dishonest. They were required to get a certain amount of money for the Roman government, but in doing so, oftentimes over-taxed their fellow Jews to make a profit for themselves. This practice was well known throughout the land. It is no coincidence that the terms *tax collector, sinner* and *outcast* often appear together. To be a tax collector most certainly put you on the outside of the rest of society. Perhaps

Zacchaeus claimed to be happy with his life the way it was, with money and property but no friends; but I doubt it. My guess is that Zacchaeus was not a happy man, that he was looking for a way to be a part of *the group*; that he wished his life were different and that he was willing to do something about it to change it.

Some might assume that it was idle curiosity that brought Zacchaeus to see Jesus and that it was only after Jesus knew his name and ate with him that in fact Zacchaeus saw the light, so to speak, and changed his life. However, there are a few things that don't make sense in the story if that were the case. *Why would an adult man try so hard to see Jesus if he were nothing more than a curiosity to him?* And when he could not see over the crowd *why would this adult run the risk of ridicule and run ahead and climb a tree in order to see him?*

Once a person became an adult in that part of the world they did not run because it was undignified. Yet we are told that this little man *ran* ahead of the group and climbed into a tree. And, by the way, the kind of tree that he must have climbed into was not a large tree with big branches to support him. Very few trees in that part of the world grow very large. Quite likely, Zacchaeus, this short squat man, breathing heavily from running, was teetering in a small tree as the group passed by. How could Jesus help but stop? Zacchaeus must have been a sight to behold!

The good Lord was using His sense of humor that day as the events played themselves out.

I believe Zacchaeus knew what he was doing when he went to the trouble of running after Jesus that day. He was looking to be a part of the group, even though he likely didn't know for certain what being a part of the group really meant. Notice one more thing about the scene as it was plays out. When Zacchaeus first goes to see Jesus, the crowd will not let him through to see the Messiah. Think about it for a moment. Jesus is coming to town, everyone is excited and is out to greet him. What a celebration!

But wait a minute, here comes that sinner Zacchaeus who robbed us blind in the past, and he looks as though he wants to see the Messiah. Well, I couldn't do anything to him in the past but I'll do what I can to keep him from Jesus! I picture a few in the crowd intentionally standing in his way, moving when he would move, to prevent him from seeing the Lord. If you think I exaggerate, remember we are told that he sought *to see the Lord* but could not on account of the crowd, because he was small of stature. Perhaps he had to run ahead to get away from those who would block his view of Christ.

As Jesus enters this laughable scene, I suspect he smiles even as he greets Zacchaeus by name. Christ knows who Zacchaeus is and *what he is* and says that today he is going to eat with him. To eat with another is to say to that person that you respect him and care about him. To break bread with another shows fellowship and community. Do you hear what the Lord is saying? Despite your past, you are a part of the fellowship Zacchaeus. Jesus already knows what it is that Zacchaeus has to tell him. He comes out of the tree and says, "Lord, the half of my goods I give to the poor and if I have defrauded anyone of anything I restore it fourfold (on both counts twice as much as would be legally expected of him)." Because of the language it could be that Zacchaeus is going to do these things, or it could be that he has already begun to do them because he has found Christ in his heart before he even meets Him in the flesh; Jesus tells him that *today salvation has come to this house,* and *by house he means to Zacchaeus.*

Look at the crowd and what they say. They see Zacchaeus and see an outcast, a sinner, and not as one who is saved and forgiven. Who really is on the outside looking in, Zacchaeus or the crowd? Who is acting like one who belongs to the Lord?

What we have in the story of Jesus and Zacchaeus is a directive to us all as individuals to let others in. Into our individual lives and into the collective life of the church, and especially into our relationship with God through the person of Jesus Christ.

Finding a sense of belonging is what life is all about; but I've got what might seem to be some very surprising news for you. Every one of us sometimes feels like we are on the outside, that we are being left out, that we are not important, that we are not needed, that we are not appreciated. It might be at home, at work, at school, at church... in our relationships with coworkers or family...yes, we *all* at times feel that we are not really a part of what goes on. But the reality is that we all need to belong, we all *want* to belong; and to Christ, *we all do belong.* Why do we belong? Because Jesus loves us! Jesus loves you and Jesus loves me! He bought us with a price. He paid the greatest price with His life so that we might each be saved; yet sometimes we are apt to forget.

Perhaps this day you find yourself feeling that you are on the outside of something, if so, you are not alone. Be assured that our Lord Jesus Christ does not pass us by when we need Him, but that He can reach out to us, in and through others.

God's love belongs to those who follow Him...and those who follow...*belong to Him! Amen.*

21

OUCH!

SUGGESTED READING: EZEKIEL 37:1-14

Have you ever had a moment in your life that caused you to look at a verse of Scripture in an entirely new light? Maybe your car was broken down on the side of a busy road and no one would stop to help you. All of the sudden the words of the parable of the Good Samaritan mean something more. Until that point, you always considered yourself from the perspective of those who passed by, but now you know what it was like to be the one ignored.

Maybe as a child you always played for great little league teams, winning many if not most of your games, until that year that nothing went right; you lost them all, until the final game of the year against the best team in the league. Everybody on their team looked 16 and none of your guys were over 4 feet tall, yet with faith and commitment you played your hardest and won the game. All of a sudden the story of David and Goliath made much more sense.

Well let me tell you, I had something happen to me a

few years ago, that caused me to view the passage from Ezekiel 37:1-14 in a completely different light than I ever did before. In fact, I am now almost positive that most, if not all the sermons ever preached on this passage of scripture have missed an essential element of this story that I now understand all too well! Let me explain.

It is important to understand that for many years I played for the church softball team. Having been gifted by God with *cat-like reflexes* and *a healthy fear of getting hit in the face by balls,* I regularly played first base the majority of the time. OK, maybe not catlike reflexes, but at least the ability to stand upright and not trip over one's own feet on the way to the bag...that was...*until* the *accident.*

It was the playoffs of the church softball league and during one of the early games, I was on second base with just one out. Only two weeks earlier, I had hit my first home run and had commented in church the following Sunday, how surprised I was as I rounded third base, that the coach gave me the sign to keep running. Amazingly, I made it home safely that day.

So on this evening, with one out, a fly ball was hit to centerfield. Bolstered by my own late season play (yes, a hero in my own mind), I went back to second base with the intent of tagging up and moving to third. The ball was caught...and I ran...as only a 20 pound overweight 42 year old minister could run. The ball was thrown to third; I slid, extending my left leg, knowing I would hit the bag and it would go flying, and of course I would be safe.

Then it happened...or should I say...it didn't happen! Oh, the thrown ball and the slide both occurred. The part that didn't was the bag at third base moving. You see on this particular field, unlike all the others we played on, the bases are fixed into the ground. I swear with three feet deep poles sunk in cement (or at least that's how it felt).

Anyway, I slid...the leg hit the bag and the bag didn't move. It was like sliding into a brick wall! It hurt. It really hurt for a second or two. Even worse was the fact that the umpire called me out...which was not right...*I was safe*... but that's beside the point.

I smacked the ground a few times in pain and disgust, got to my feet and limped over to the bench assuming everything would be fine in a few minutes. What I didn't realize at the time was that I had completely torn my *anterior cruciate ligament* or ACL.

I came to learn that this ligament is located in the very middle of the knee and helps it rotate properly. It also keeps the tibia in place. It is one of the four ligaments in the knee that help humans walk. It works with the posterior cruciate ligament to keep the tibia stable, or at least it used to do those things, until a moment before I slid. The problem was that I didn't realize what I had done, so even though it hurt...I kept trying to play.

The next inning, I went out to play first base. A ball was hit to the infield so I went to take a step towards first to take the throw, and it was like I stepped in six foot hole in the ground. My leg completely gave way and I fell flat on my face. Now, I not only had the pain of my injury but the embarrassment of not being able to do the one thing a softball first baseman should be able to do, put one foot in front of the other and stand on the base.

Over the next several weeks, I dealt with several more types of pain. First came the pain of denial as my wife, Karen, would tell me "you need to get your leg looked at... I think something is wrong...you really need to go to the doctor...you can't limp around like that forever." My response, "Just give it a little more time...I'll put another ace bandage on it...I'll be fine."

Eventually, I gave in, had the tests done and saw the pictures of what *wasn't there* in my leg. The first week of November, I had surgery to attach a new ligament inside my knee, a procedure that does not take particularly long (taking a piece of ligament from one part of your body and putting it in another.) It doesn't take long, but it does hurt! That's right. There is not only pain when ligaments are torn. There is even *greater pain* when they are *reattached!*

That wasn't the end of the pain however. Over the next several months, there was pain involved in the physical therapy I was doing, pushing myself to bend more, stretch more and to put more weight on the leg. Eventually my strength began to return.

How excited I was when the doctor and physical therapist both said, "You will be recovered enough to play church softball the following year! But you will need to wear a special sports brace from now on when you play." "*Fine!*" I said. I was fitted, the brace was designed, I was shown how to wear it. And then the greatest pain of all came...*the bill!* That's right the *unexpected but necessary cost.* After all, nothing is free!

I went home that afternoon to tell Karen. I pointed out that the brace cost more than my first car did. She added that it was more than her wedding dress, which I thought was silly because I couldn't wear her wedding dress to play softball anyway. Over a 10 month span I experienced a variety of pains and challenges; in fact the leg still hurts at times, many years later, and believe me, I am *still* paying.

These are the days of Ezekiel,
The dry bones becoming as flesh;
I will lay sinews on you, and will cause flesh to come upon
you and cover you with skin and put breath in you and you
shall live and you shall know that I am the Lord.

This passage has an individual and collective message to it. Collectively, it speaks of God taking the remnants that are dead and making them to be His people in all their splendor and blessings. Individually, it says to the listener that renewal and revival of the spirit, is in fact possible, even when life seems its darkest.

The meaning we can take from this is that our situation is never hopeless. God is constantly wanting to breathe new life into dry bones. Do we sometimes feel like dry bones, like there is no joy left, that everything we try fails and God seems to be nowhere? Then God has the power to restore new life. By saying *these are the days,* we are saying that God is moving among us, that the time of dryness is at an end and that God is doing something *new* and *life bringing,* among us.

Why does God do this? Well, I am reminded of the story of the minister whose neighbor's cat was run over by a car. The mother quickly disposed of the remains before her four-year-old son, Billy, found out about it. After a few days, though, Billy finally asked about the cat.

"Billy, the cat died," his mother explained, "But it's all right. He's up in heaven with God."

The boy asked, "What in the world would God want with a *dead cat?*"

What in the world would God want with dry bones? The spiritually dead? We need a spiritual awakening! Our bones are dry. There are many people, in the world and in church, who have dry bones, who are spiritually dead, who need to hear the Word of the Lord, and for the Lord to awaken and breathe new life into their bones! Almost every sermon I have ever heard or read regarding this passage of scripture has a title like...*Hope!...All's Well that Ends Well...The knee bone's connected to the thigh bone*...etc. They are all warm, fuzzy, happy images. There is a problem though. They seem to ignore, or gloss over, the fact that something happened. Something *bad* happened to cause those bones to be dry in the first place, and secondly, it really hurts to reattach ligaments to bones! It quite literally is a pain!

Sin is a devastating word. Sin is so devastating and unbearable that our society has tried to get rid of that word. Today's world has turned sin into diseases. So-called experts have renamed sin. *God still considers sin as sin.* Worse, our world has, at times, tried to ignore sin, deny sin, or act like sin does not even exist. But that is not what God's Word says. "Everyone has turned away, they have together become corrupt; there is no one who does good, not even one" (Psalm 53:3). Everyone is included in the utter hopelessness that sin brings.

Sin hurts us...when we lie, cheat, steal, bear false witness, *whatever*...it hurts us. Like that slide into third...we don't even realize how much at times. Eventually, however, it separates us from one another and even disconnects us from our God. Like I tried to do with my knee; we can pretend it's fine, we aren't hurting. But then we need to act...and fall flat on our face.

Even if we are *ready, willing and able* to turn from our sinful ways with God's help, we need to recognize there will still be pain. So many Bibles and Bible Studies like to emphasize that this passage of scripture demonstrates how *God graciously restores hope*...and that's all well and good, but don't mistake *gracious* with pain free.

There is pain in change! Just as surgery and rehab are painful but necessary, if a person is to grow strong again, we need to acknowledge that there is pain in turning from our sinful ways. Ask the alcoholic or drug addict who has gone cold turkey, the man or woman who can no longer associate with former friends who continue to participate in illicit activities, the person who must change jobs because they have a moral objection to what is being done in the business.

Turning from sin is painful. And it's not done in an instant. It takes time. Like physical therapy, it is a process. To keep going in the right way that God intends takes effort...but, *no pain, no gain!*

Lastly, and most importantly, is the *price!* The *cost* to be remade in the image of God, the *price* in being made whole once more. The *price* for dry bones to become as flesh is the greatest of all; in fact it's so much that we can't even afford it. We cannot pay it alone.

If we did anything to merit our salvation, we would be forever boasting about it in heaven. The fact is that we could do nothing, so Jesus paid it all. The price was paid on a cross at Calvary. It was there our Savior bore that pain so that we might be reconnected, reattached to our God.

The reality is that you and I, and true believers everywhere, worship a God unlike any other god. We have sinned and we deserve eternal punishment. Our heavenly Father sends His Son, Jesus, to die in our place and give us eternal life. We turn against God and others with a multitude of sinful thoughts, words, and actions. God turns to us in His mercy and brings us back by His free grace and forgiveness. When our lives are broken, the Great Physician can reconnect us, make us whole and make us one with Him. We are no longer lost in the utter hopelessness of sin. By God's free grace He restores hope—now and forever. *Amen.*

22

TEACH YOUR CHILDREN WELL

SUGGESTED READING: II TIMOTHY 3:14-4:5

Teach your children well. But be careful that you are clear about what it is you desire for them to learn. I learned this lesson the hard way when our four children were quite young. I remember it like it was yesterday, although it has now been twenty years. Our three older children (John, Aaron and Annie) were playing together roughhousing and laughing, while their then, year and half old brother, Joshua, sat crying in a corner.

I was sitting in our family room reading the newspaper at the time and noticed what was taking place. I proceeded to set down the paper, called the three older children over and explained, "Didn't you hear mommy and daddy say that you were supposed to play with Joshua?" "OK," they replied, while escorting Joshua out of the room.

Assuming the minor crisis had passed, I picked up my paper and began to read once more. A moment or two later I was startled as Joshua came running through one door of the family room and out the other, arms waving in the air, laughing and screaming. Right behind him were his older sister and two brothers, running with a stick, a broom and a whiffle ball bat, chasing him!

Of course I grabbed them immediately and asked what they were doing, to which they responded…"you told us to play with Joshua, so we're using him to play baby piñata!"

I had told them to play with their brother, but not exactly *how* to play with him. Once I did, their excuse was, "*we didn't know that is what you meant daddy?*"

The reality is that we live in a world of *excuse makers*. A world in which anytime that we are confronted with something that we have done or left undone, the only response necessary is "I didn't know."

Whether it be a little child who conveniently forgets to clean up their room…"*I didn't know I was supposed to do it*"…or a teenager who forgets to do their homework,…"*I didn't know I had any to do*"…to the adult who gets caught driving forty miles per hour in a twenty-five mile per hour zone…."*I didn't know what the speed limit was, officer.*"

We love to make excuses. Nothing is ever our fault. If I didn't know that I was supposed to do something…then it's not really my fault when I don't. Or at least this is the argument we make for our actions or lack thereof.

The problem is that this attitude is not in any way new to human beings today. It has been prevalent since the very beginning of time.

If you make a habit of exceeding the speed limit in your car, and you get a ticket for speeding, for a while thereafter, you take great care to drive within the limit. But as time passes and you forget the pain of paying that ticket, you begin to press the pedal to the floor just a little bit further, until you are right back to where you were before the ticket.

As time passes, we forget what we have been told and go back to doing and acting the way we desire with little to no thought given as to what the consequences might be. The tone of the letter to Timothy has in mind this very characteristic of human nature.

Whether the letter was written by Paul, or those who followed him, the realization was that as time passed there would be challenges and difficulties that would arise in the lives of believers. It was foreseen that followers would face a time during which the faithful would be persecuted and the faithless would become more notorious.

In other words, the further one got away from the time of Jesus and the Words of Christ, the more likely it would be that the believer would *forget* what he or she believed and they would, in turn, be tempted away from the faith. Little has changed in our world today. Time and circumstance have led us away from the Word of God.

Read again what Paul said in his letter:

"The time is coming when people will not put up with sound doctrine, but having itching ears, they will accumulate for themselves teachers to suit their own desires and will turn away from listening to the truth and wander away to myths."

Our growing reliance on the internet and social media are partially but not exclusively responsible for causing us to *wander.* We have convinced ourselves that "if Google says it…it must be true!" We find answers to questions that fit our preconceived notions and rarely challenge ourselves to learn something new by thinking "outside the box." We follow news services that *spin* the news the direction we prefer (both left and right) and in the process grow further and further apart as a society. Some might claim that, as a people, we are no longer *wandering,* but rather *running away* to myths in search of answers to life's problems.

In the meantime, more and more often we see persons of faith ridiculed by the media. We watch as efforts are regularly made to remove God from the public stage and the political process. Why do you suppose, when we need God most in our lives, our world, and our society, do we seem to be relying upon Him less and less?

Some would blame the anti-religious of this world; those who are openly hostile to matters of faith and to those who claim to believe them. I, on the other hand, believe the blame lies much closer to home with those who claim to believe and yet do not really follow! How many claim the title "Christian" and yet do not really believe in living a life of faith as being all that fundamental to who we are and the lives we live.

I find it quite telling that if our cable goes out, within five or ten minutes we place a call to the company to have it fixed, because we know we can't live without television. If our WIFI goes down we grow more irritated by the second and if someone takes away our cell phone, we practically lose our mind! Yet, it's been over fifty years (1962) since they took prayer out of school, have you made your call about *that* yet? Why not? "Because I didn't know it would matter...I didn't think it made a difference."

The problem with the world is not all those sinful people outside the church who have never heard of or accepted Christ. The problem with the world today is with those who call themselves Christians, who claim to be the church, and yet do little or nothing about it.

And the letter to Timothy confirms this...and that is why what is said is said: "*Continue in what you have learned and firmly believed, knowing from whom you learned it, and how from childhood you have known the sacred writings that are able to instruct you for salvation through faith in Christ Jesus."*

In other words, those who have heard the message, who have heard the word; *we are the ones* who must *continue in the faith.* Otherwise all is lost.

This is a critical time in which we live. We like to sit around and bemoan the fact that fewer and fewer people take religion seriously. One of the biggest complaints we have is that young people don't have a religious connection...*young people don't come to church, the younger generation just doesn't care!* To this, I say "you are exactly right," but I would add, it's not their fault it is OURS...we who call ourselves *the church* and yet do little or nothing about it. Remember what Paul said?

"Continue in what you have learned and firmly believed, knowing from whom you learned it, and how from childhood you have known the sacred writings that are able to instruct you for salvation through faith in Christ Jesus."

There was a reason your grandmother told you to say your prayers every night before you went to bed, there was a reason your parents made you get up and go to church each Sunday even when you didn't want to. And you know what? It made a difference in your life!

Continue what you learned from your childhood!

We live in a society today that is filled with people; young and old, who do not know the Lord, and only *we* can do something about it.

Instead of sitting back and bemoaning the state of the world from behind the perceived safety of our church walls, we should be taking it to the Lord in prayer. But we don't because we don't really believe that our life in Christ is all that essential. We are oftentimes an apathetic people, and we had better get over it fast, before it's too late, for others out in the world, and for us in the church.

The work of being faithful and committed is difficult. The likelihood is that many will respond that they "didn't know" what they were supposed to do. Fortunately II Timothy offers some very sound advice for everyone who believes!

First, *"Proclaim the message"*! It's a simple one: *"For God so loved the world that He gave His only begotten son that whosoever believes in Him should not perish but have eternal life." (John 3:16)*

Secondly *"Be persistent whether the time is favorable or unfavorable."* You say, "But my neighbors think I'm a fanatic, my kids say I'm bugging them and my spouse just never listens to me."

No one said it was easy. Only that we must try. The need for people to hear about Christ is now, and the perfect time may never come along, so what better time to start than now!

And thirdly, *"Convince, rebuke and encourage, with the utmost patience in teaching."*

I know how frustrating it can be. It might, in fact, take years of encouraging and convincing before God ultimately does the convicting of another's life, but what happens if we don't do our part?

Ask yourself, how convincing a picture does my life paint of what a relationship with Jesus Christ means?

When our oldest son John Wesley was four or five, he would sit with me and we would watch professional football and hockey together. As soon as he sat down John would ask the same question: "Which is our team?" I would tell him and then he would ask, "What are the bad guy's names?"

John knew that we are the good guys and so obviously the other team must be the bad guys.

What we have forgotten in the church, is that we are the good guys, or at least we are supposed to be, and we have a responsibility to act as part of that team to defeat the enemy.

Timothy is told, *always be sober, endure suffering, do the work of an evangelist, carry out your ministry fully.* That is the command to every person of faith as well. Note that I did not say that is was a suggestion, a word of encouragement, or even a choice. As followers of Christ we are commanded to do certain things; it is our responsibility. It is not an option, and until we understand that, nothing will change.

"Love the Lord your God with all your heart, soul, mind, and strength and your neighbor as yourself. Go into all the world and make disciples. Teach them to obey everything I have commanded you..."

Remember that the Scriptures tell us that *all Scripture is inspired by God for teaching so everyone may be equipped for every good work.*

These are teachings we cannot afford to overlook. We are called as children of God, to share the love of Christ with others and bring them to the Lord, you can call it love, you can call it caring, you can call it evangelism, you can call it bugging...call it whatever you like, but in order to serve our Lord...we must do it.

Let us teach our children well. Not to be makers of excuses, but to actively live and share the Word. No excuses. We owe it to our children and to all of God's children. We can do no less. *Amen*!

PART IV DISCUSSION QUESTIONS

1. Are you a front porch or backyard person?
2. How does a life in Christ help to alleviate worry in one's life?
3. When have you felt that you were on the *outside*? How did those *inside* reach out to you and bring you back in?
4. When it comes to growing in our relationship with Christ, what do you think of the adage *no pain, no gain!?*
5. Ask yourself, "What *have I learned from others that I will share in the future?*

ABOUT THE AUTHOR

Mark Hecht grew up in the little central Pennsylvania town of Duncansville. His family roots as well as the friendships he made there continue to influence him to this day. His educational route took him to Allegheny College, Pittsburgh Theological Seminary and Wesley Seminary. He has served 30 plus years as an ordained minister and preacher in a wide variety of churches, from the inner city to small towns.

In addition to the local church, Mark has worked as a hospice chaplain and professor of church history at several universities. All of these places and experiences proved to be fertile ground for developing his deep sense of appreciation for the sometimes ordinary events through which God chooses to work. Mark and his wife of thirty-one years, Karen have four adult children. Mark currently serves in Warren, PA.

57111735R00123

Made in the USA
Middletown, DE
27 July 2019